POETRY ESCAPE

Break the silence,
tell your truth.

POETS FROM THE SOUTH EAST

Edited By Kelly Reeves

First published in Great Britain in 2019 by:

Young Writers

Young Writers
Remus House
Coltsfoot Drive
Peterborough
PE2 9BF
Telephone: 01733 890066
Website: www.youngwriters.co.uk

FOREWORD

Since 1991 our aim here at Young Writers has been to encourage creativity in children and young adults and to inspire a love of the written word. Each competition is tailored to the relevant age group, hopefully giving each student the inspiration and incentive to create their own piece of creative writing, whether it's a poem or a short story. We truly believe that seeing their work in print gives students a sense of achievement and pride.

For our latest competition *Poetry Escape*, we challenged secondary school students to free their creativity and break through the barriers to express their true thoughts, using poetic techniques as their tools of escape. They had several options to choose from offering either a specific theme or a writing constraint. Alternatively they could forge their own path, because there's no such thing as a dead end where imagination is concerned.

The result is an inspiring anthology full of ideas, hopes, fears and imagination, proving that creativity really does offer escape, in whatever form you need it.

We encourage young writers to express themselves and address topics that matter to them, which sometimes means exploring sensitive or difficult topics. If you have been affected by any issues raised in this book, details on where to find help can be found at: **www.youngwriters.co.uk/support**.

CONTENTS

Maplesden Noakes School, Great Buckland

Hannah Irving (13)	84
Esther Gardner (13)	86
Charlotte Rickard (14)	87
Meredith King (14)	88
April Shanahan (13)	90
Libby Rogers (12)	92
Isobel Browning (13)	94
Holly Irving (16)	96
Francesca Thomas (15)	98
Harry Spain (14)	99
Alexander Coulton (14)	100

Robert Clack School, Dagenham

Adrian Simmons (15)	101

Robert Clack School Of Science, Dagenham

Yasmin Cabak (14)	102
Jaynell Prempeh (13)	107
Persis George (14)	108
Jackie Bukari (14)	111
Romeo Osei-Nyarko (13)	112
Youhans Dilloo (14)	114
Harley Browning (13)	116
Alok Bhogal (14)	118
Christopher Browne Maddox (13)	120
Thinuja Thileepan (14)	122
Tisha Rahman (14)	124
Jeehaan Dilloo (14)	126
Mary Ansong (14)	128
Kalista Serdiukovaite (14)	130
Neha Samplay (14)	132
Minahil Ubaid (14)	134
Ellie-Kay Joan Taylor (14)	136
Akash Nath (13)	138
Caitlin Davies (13)	139
Sarah Haxell (14)	140
Muneeb Musharaf (14)	142

Rand Ali Basha (14)	143
Ahed Umair Gardaizi (14)	144
Charlie Cape (14)	146
Imad Ahmed (14)	147
Logan Allen (14)	148
Rida Syeda Noor (13)	150
Lacey Summer Tier (14)	151
Endri Halili (14)	152
Umar Khilji (14)	153
Thomas Webb (14)	154
Dipo Eweoya (13)	155
Jessica Cook (13)	156
Joseph Palmer (14)	157
Chloe Brooks (14)	158
Freddy Joe Ling (13)	159
Kyle Irving (14)	160

St Edward's CE School & Sixth Form College, Romford

Ashleen Mpambawahle (13)	161
Ogechi G Ugoji (13)	162
Keziah Edward (12)	164

St John The Baptist School, Kingfield

Jesse Ayres (11)	165
Oliwia Ziemak (11)	166
Elani Isabella Bidessie-Mistretta (12)	169
Poppy Phin (11)	170
Ella Browne-Kaempf (11)	172
Kathleen D'Costa (12)	174
Yzabella Laguisma (11)	176
Sophia Bocer (12)	178
Teresa Sanchez (12)	181
Catherine Henn (11)	182
Sofia Lorraine Sarao (12)	184
William Ezzard (12)	186
Kristian Guardiana (12)	188
Keira Borlagdatan (11)	190
Freya Willis (11)	192
Rosina Waplington (12)	194

The Judd School, Tonbridge

THE POEMS

The Sinister Winter

It is a very dark and stormy night,
It is too windy for a kite.
The houses are a dark silhouette,
Everyone is playing games with a headset.

The dark passages are scary and gloomy,
There is no one there so it is rather roomy.
The mother of all storms is coming,
With the thunder completely drumming.

By the sea, there is a house on a hill,
Down by the sea, there is such a chill.
The house is towering and tall,
Making all the other houses seem like a tiny ball.

There is a man who is very mysterious,
He always seems rather serious.
The storm changes people,
So watch out as it is lethal.

Connor Schneider-Smith
Ashford School, Ashford

What She Tried To Fight

Dear insecurities,

I try to hide my problems,
I bury them and put on a fake smile,
It works, my hurt is disguised, I praise others,
I want them to feel loved,
I don't want them to feel like me,
I don't want anyone to feel alone.

I want to hide,
Lock up my feelings, thoughts, my torture,
People say that when words fail,
You can always count on the eyes to speak,
Then why am I still alone?
I want to cry, cry for help.

I sleep,
My true self takes control,
I dream of all the broken butterflies,
Their wings torn against life's thorn,
I understand the pain,
The pain they've undergone,
Dreaming... it's less full of tragedy,
And more full of someone else's pain.

I don't want to rouse, I can take a nightmare,
In it, I don't feel,
But when it ends...

I'm transported into a new nightmare,
A real one, where I can feel,
I'm in a nightmare that conceals itself,
It's disguised as a normal teenager's life...

But I'm not normal,
No one normal would feel happy, happy when drenched,
Drenched in red, red blood, of their own,
No one normal would scar themselves just to feel alive,
No one normal would pour out bullets from their eyes,
Every day...
Drip! Drop! Drip! Drop!
Every time a tear rolls off my cheek, it falls, and so do I,
I fall deeper into my handmade pit of misery,
But no one sees,
No one notices just how I far I've fallen,
Or just how lost I feel...

I'm lost in myself, I can't breathe...
All I can hear is... talk! Just say something! Talk!
I don't want to...
I want to scream!
But I can't, would anyone?
No one would be able to
If their demons were crushing their lungs,
I don't want to be saved; all I need is someone there,
Someone to stand by me through it all,
I want to try... try to save myself,

I know I could fail, I could fall,
But I believe if I find that someone, they'll save me,
So I can try again.

But all the jokes, shoves, trips, fiendish smirks,
They outweigh the reasons to live,
I've been robbed of everything,
I don't have emotions, a voice, a mind...
But I have a heart,
I have a half-devoured, unamendable, worthless heart,
A heart in a terrible condition,
I'll take anything!
But... please take my heart,
Please cut it out of my chest,
Free my soul,

And end my suffering...

Aysha Ali (13)
Ayesha Siddiqa Girls' School, Southall

Love

A thing we don't have in this world,
A thing most people call a label,
To think leaving kids to swallow the hollow emptiness of
poverty is love,
And to let teens suffer from endless bullying, suicide and
depression,
A prick of blood dropped from a bruised heart,
No first aid can patch it up,
For some, the only cure is death.

Love
A thing most people struggle to find,
A person is put into a category for his race.
You think that's love?

Battered with pain,
An empty void lives in your belly,
The only cure is love,
A thing I will never find.
For a void lives in my soul and will never be filled,
'Cause only an insane person will make me feel welcome
In a world I'll never belong in.

Classes are a dungeon for doom,
Kids going to school, hungry like their anguished cries at
night.
For some, the only cure is death,
And that was my cure...

Aisha Omar (12)
Ayesha Siddiqa Girls' School, Southall

Breakthrough

Hate?
Is there a median?
When used to something
Pain is numbed.

By the sweetness
It easily flows through
Cracks
Filled until the sun arrives.

Night night
Sleep tight
Don't let them...
Bite
But doesn't tightness
Suffocate?
Legs of their own
Do they stop?
Bug bites?
They pierce!
Head to heart
Condensing on the toes
Cold feet
Red eyes.

Light arrives
Blinding

Control...
Out of control
Dead end.

You know
It's nothing
A smile is just a line on your face
Stretch it
You can mould anything
Like moulding clay
Books are too long
I guess a person is longer.

Rushing the rest
Time is short
Light arrives
Blinding.
No cupcakes and rainbows
Tattoos on the body
Perhaps tattoos would be better.

It's all in the head
Control, control...
No control.

I speak to myself
'Cause no one else will
I crack glass
Due to selfish reflections

Then I stare...

Control, control...
Control...
No control.

My friend's here
Although dark, he shines
The lines begin to mould
But...

Knock knock!
Another guest?
No more guests!

I'm the mom!
I'm the dad!
Comfort is by me
Change...
Is by me.

Positivity?
Meh
Rethink
'After hardship comes ease'.

Motivation! Happiness!
Cupcakes and rainbows!
Impossible...

'After hardship comes ease'.

Motivation! Happiness!
Cupcakes and rainbows!

No more colour blindness!
No more knocks late at night!
Friends in the day
Friends in the night
They both shine so bright!

Control, control...
Control, control...
Control!

Maisha Siddika (16)
Ayesha Siddiqa Girls' School, Southall

Labels

That's just how it is
What did you miss?
'Cause that's what society calls us
Why is it that I don't make a fuss?
You have a label
But it's unstable
White, black, ugly or pretty
Alright, mental, weird or witty

But that's wrong!
It doesn't matter whether I'm young
Why are we all friends and foes?
We wait, awaiting our foe's two last blows
But why?
Do you really wanna die?
We live on this Earth
Straight from birth
Until we die
Without saying goodbye.

Why do you kill one another?
Aren't we sisters or brothers?
Fathers or mothers?
Sons or daughters?
Grandfathers or grandmothers?
At this rate
Are we gonna call our friends 'mate'?

It's just a label
Pretty unstable
There are people sufferin' every day
Every minute
Every millennium
Bad thoughts flickering into my head
Coming with me, right into my bed
Telling me, "You're not worthy to live
Kill yourself on a boat, just dive."
I was victimised, I was bullied
By myself.

One day, I felt like my life was over
Did I have anything left over?
I hanged myself
Do not do this yourself
It had nothing to do with health
Neither to do with wealth
I thought life was blue
Did I have a clue?
I left behind the place I once called home
I left behind the thing in the garden I once called a gnome
I left behind the woman I once called Mother
I left behind the man I once called Father
For now, I am alone
Forsaken and forlorn
I regret what I have done
I miss my home, dad and mom

Under the fresh soil, I was dug in
My life and hard work put in a bin
For that was the end of my life
Goodbye!

Siham Abdi Shire (11)
Ayesha Siddiqa Girls' School, Southall

A Girl With Dreams

I'm a human
With a heart,
But most of all,
I have feelings,
But I'm different,
At least,
That's what they all say,
They call me names,
Every single day,
As I walk out,
I think,
Be myself,
Be unique,
Be me,
I look in the mirror,
I see a girl,
A heartbroken girl,
An unhappy girl,
A girl with *dreams*,
Dreams that keep her alive,
Dreams that tell her,
She'll be happy once more,
But until then,
I'll keep dreaming,
'Til my *dreams* become reality.

Saidiya Moalin (13)
Ayesha Siddiqa Girls' School, Southall

Maculinidad Toxica - Virtilite Toxique - Toxic Masculinity

Toxic like acid, but much deeper
Than what acid can penetrate.
It devours man's heart in order
To reiterate what has been echoed in one's mind.

It suppresses natural feelings, such as to cry
To grieve in a time of despair -
This feeling does not allow you to put your ego aside!
It is a constant reminder to man
That he must live by the 'rules' and that 'real men don't cry',
But in reality, they're human, just like us females.

Conditioned from a young age to be 'extra polite' to the ladies,
Expressing emotions is a 'no go'
'Man up', what a deluding phrase,
Ingrained in the minds of young, innocent boys
Who have yet to find themselves.
It is a disguise from the roots
Of the bigger construct of society's intentions.
It hits deeper within the vessels that pulsates through man,
It sabotages their own future by being 'tough' and emotionally detached.

The cult so toxic...
You cannot leave it.

If you do, you're ostracised and isolated,
The toxic society no longer accepts you,
The 'normal' no longer mingle with you,
The 'natural' environments you were so used to
Suddenly appears so wrong and deluding.
No sympathy thrown your way because
You are now labelled as 'the guy with emotions',
Your mind reshaping, remoulding itself,
To get rid of this foolish ideology that 'real men don't cry'
Or that 'men need to be emotionally available for women',
But not vice versa.

To that I say, "Out with the old, in with the new."
But there will never be an escape from the shackles of man.

Zainab Aliat Adeyemi (15)
Ayesha Siddiqa Girls' School, Southall

The Race To Good Grades

My delicate hands crack like leather
Into rigid, scratched claws
And my brain spins like clockwork.
Pumped with violently fizzing nourishment,
Sold in packs of six bottles -
It latches onto my throat, bubbling ferociously,
But I shake my head,
How on earth will I survive otherwise?

Bound to a race against time,
In the forest, agony but I try,
My pulse quickens; where is the finish line?

Panting, I frantically speed up
As jagged razor-sharp stones
Pierce through my trembling ankles.
I take a gulp of air and bear the excruciating pain,
They say without it, there'd be no gain,
But why was I forced to be a part of this race?

Struggling,
Raw, salty tears stinging my eyes,
I drag and trudge forward,
Come on, come on, come on...

"Come on!"
I burst awake, my head gyrates,
I see blinding, vivid colour

Like flickering images on a cinema screen,
Where am I?
"Oh come on, that's the third time this month!"
I look up steadily and I see
A disappointed English teacher and a place
I've already seen.

Bound to a race against time,
Ink to paper, dash, underline,
Their pulse quickens, crying,
"It's almost the finish time."

"Don't forget, mocks are in two weeks!"
I see bloodshot eyes share a hopeless ache.
"No time to be sleeping, I don't care if you're weak."

I lean back in my chair, beaming with glee,
Like an amber, hazy sunset.
I have completed the task early
And with a fifteen-minute break;
For a moment, I am able to escape.

Raheema Asim (15)
Ayesha Siddiqa Girls' School, Southall

The Flip Side

What is war?
It is the flip side
We do we sit and abide?
Continuously accepting that there are people who are
suffering
But we don't do anything to stop the numbering
Bodies building and piling
But we just sit here and start the tiling
Of the guilt that builds up inside of us
Because we know it's our duty to fuss
Not just sit here and discuss
And question thus:

What is war?
When there are millions dying in front of us
As we sit and enjoy our school bus
That takes us to a place of education
Which is the future of our nation
But we forget our obligation
To our fellow human creation.

Who are in the flip side?
The place on the other ship side
The place where abominable things happen
Where people's homes have become misshapen
A place where education is a privilege
Because of the bodies that build like points in cribbage.

You see, what is the purpose of education?
If we are not taught the foundation
The key to this world's progress
A statement that will help us transgress:

Every little counts
Every little thing mounts
Into a way of helping others
Our fellow sisters and brothers
But again, you can question
What is war?
Is it the epitome of human nature's destruction?
Or a lesson in how to begin reconstruction
From the mistakes that we as humankind have made in the past?
So that the question is not again asked
What is war?

Zahrah Fatima Azeem (16)
Ayesha Siddiqa Girls' School, Southall

Only Person On Earth

I feel like the only person on Earth,
No one can help me, since birth,
But everyone can break me, death.

People say you shouldn't be here,
But sometimes, I say to myself, "They're not clear."

They judge me by my face,
They judge me by my race,
But do they know what I go through on a daily basis?

I have struggles at home,
I have struggles at school,
Where don't I have struggles?
I ask myself, don't you?

The saying goes, 'Sticks and stones may break my bones
But words will never hurt me'
But I feel like the saying really is, 'Sticks and stones
Break my bones and words will forever hurt me'.

I have no friends,
I feel like the only person on Earth,
No one can help me,
Buy everyone can break me.
I know it's really hard
Feeling like the odd one out, position,
Can I ask you a question?

Are you yourself around people?
Do you just try to fit into a sequel?

I know it's really difficult...
But there is somebody out there who can help anyone...
God!

Everywhere you go, you feel like there is no happiness
But I promise you,
You'll find the place that comforts you the most
Between the words of God.

I don't feel like the only person on Earth,
Everyone can help me,
But no one can break me.

Fatima Nori (12)
Ayesha Siddiqa Girls' School, Southall

Questions

There was once a girl who asked herself a question,
"Am I beautiful like they said in the lesson?"
"Yes," said a voice, "you are very iridescent."
So she went on with her day, without the slightest
depression.

Another girl asked herself the same thing,
"Am I beautiful? Am I slim?"
"No," said a voice, "you are not thin."
"Then I must not eat anything."

And so, she did not eat dinner,
But she continued to grow thinner.
The aurora around her grew dimmer
Because she never knew that the voice was a killer.

There was once a boy who asked himself something,
"Am I strong? Or is that just a theory?"
"You are not strong," said a voice, "do not try to pull
fakery."
"Then I must obtain victory."

And so, he worked himself to the bone,
Either at school or at home,
He said he could not be broken by sticks or stones,
But he always felt pain, it just wouldn't show.

Although some people do not struggle, others do,

They also feel pain too,
Whether they are Muslim, Christian, or Hindu,
Try to get them out of the blues.

Amina Raja (11)
Ayesha Siddiqa Girls' School, Southall

Expectations

Expectations...
Society's expectations will be the death of me
This is not what it feels like to be free
Am I living? Or just existing?

There's this cloud that follows me around
But hush girl, don't make a sound
It's better to let yourself drown...

We're always fighting
Trying to be the best
There's no such thing as rest
Just stress
To be the best
Because these are the expectations!

You're expected to look, act and dress a certain way
They say smile when you're feeling a little grey
Just to tear it down
Over and over and over again...

Mental health isn't rain
You can't just pour it down the drain
Why is society so vain?

These chains are so straining
All these marks and likes I'm not gaining...

I see my personality shaping into society's expectations

This is only the foundation
Society's expectations will be the death of me.

Anaum Malik (15)
Ayesha Siddiqa Girls' School, Southall

Escape

Society isn't just fun and games,
It can hurt when they give you many names,
"You need to be the best!"
"I really just want to rest..."

These expectations are too high,
"Come back after you straighten your tie!"
"Is this your grade?"
Heartbroken, I feel betrayed...

A little birdie told me,
"If you want to be free,
You need to find the key..."

Mahabuba Rahman (12)
Ayesha Siddiqa Girls' School, Southall

One Voice

Have you ever been bullied into submission?
No one really wants to listen,
I swear that this is like long division,
I look up in the sky, tears streaming down my eyes.
I stay up all night, gazing at the sunrise.
Why do you lie?
I despise when you lie,
I'm on the road to say bye,
So I can just fly high.
Why can't you just be a good guy?
I'm crying every day 'cause of this black eye,
You're like an undercover spy.
One can change the world,
One voice can be heard,
And together, we can make the world better,
Create smiles and happy energy.

Sanel Haktan (14)
Chace Community School, Enfield

Think

Spreading lies,
Corrupting lives,
It camouflages justice,
It conceals your injustice.

You dishonour the Internet,
You make them feel regret,
They take down their picture,
Making you feel richer.

Manipulating the playground,
You send those to the ground,
It goes on after the bell,
You make their lives hell.

You obstruct the blue rivers,
You cause those to quiver,
It is your slanderous speech,
That makes their lives bleak.

You strike without warning,
Leaving their families mourning,
The blue rivers are dried,
They can no longer cry.

If you could see what it is you do,
You too would not argue,
That what you do is malicious,

The outcome is never delicious.

You let them hang,
You let the guns go *bang*,
You let the knife cut,
You let their lives shut.

You should make their lives greater,
You should change for the better,
You should begin to share,
You should begin to care.

David Buck (14) & Adam
Chace Community School, Enfield

I Am Awake

It's 2:07am and my heart is pounding
It's the middle of the night, I am awake
I feel lonely and lost
Everyone is asleep, I am awake.

My mind is putting all of these ideas into my head, I feel worried
I am thinking about all the things that could happen to me
I'm scared to move in case the imaginary person (I think is there)
Standing outside my door sees me
The shadow hanging on my ceiling starts to sway back and forth.

I hear a knocking from downstairs that makes me jump
I slowly move to get out of bed
A car passes by my window and I think the car has stopped outside my house
I start to breathe heavily as I slowly creep towards my bedroom door.

As I start to open my door, I see the shadow on my ceiling is my dressing gown
The knocking I hear is the fridge downstairs
I hear a light switch flick and I let go of the door
It bangs against the stone, stopping it from closing
I freeze, I remember the study light makes a sound.

My heart feels like it's thudding at 100 miles per hour

I start to remember all the noises and sounds my house makes
My heart relaxes a bit now, I am awake.

I poke my head out of the door
I am struggling to see because the light on the landing is very bright
I cautiously step out of the door, keeping my eyes peeled for my surroundings
Creeping up the stairs as silently as I can towards Mum and Dad's bedroom
I peer into the bathroom, checking that no one is there.

I tiptoe towards Mum's side of the bed, knowing she is there
I crouch down beside her and watch her sleeping
I think, *she is sleeping peacefully and not worrying*
I whisper quietly, "Mum." She doesn't move
I whisper again and this time she wakes up.

Lying in bed, we listen to the noises together
They sound the same
In the day, they are still there, but I don't hear them
Everyday noises drown them out
In the night, they are still there, nothing has changed
I can still hear them, but I know they are just the noises in my house.

Happy thoughts fill my head
I am asleep...

Ellen Rousell (11)
Hove Park School, Hove

I Wish We Could Live In A Time Like This

The net consumes us all, especially teens,
Detaching us from the outside world,
They do not know what is going on outside the Internet,
Only Instagram and Snapchat updates,
The mind will drown without any help.

Halfway around the world,
WaterAid begs for help,
Though hardly anyone from the west is bothered to help,
Only those who have experienced the trouble and pain,
But still, where is the food to feed the villages,
The education for the children?
Where are they?

Rights for women,
That's been on the news,
Though we still struggle so much,
In countries like Iran,
They used to flourish with life,
Double decks were a thing you know,
But now, no girl can show their hair or leave the country,
Without asking their father or husband,
And that unfair society continues.
In other countries, girls don't go to school,
They lose all the skills they would have had after graduation,

And still, that unfair system continues.

War is everywhere,
It never leaves,
It's in our blood and begins with our behaviour and the
things that we do,
But do we really need all this bloodshed?
What good does it bring us?
All it brings is blood and death,
No happiness comes from it.

For years, the planet has crumbled,
In a few years, nothing will be left,
For years now, we have ignored the signs,
That our fragile planet is dying,
Trees tumble, oil extracted,
In the air, the clouds, the atmosphere,
Pollutants fill them all.

I wish we could live in a time,
Where peace is everywhere,
With no war and no poverty,
With women's rights and where no one is put down,
And where the Internet will not consume people,
But inspire them more every day,
For people to be more active and there be more
opportunities for all,
Where the sea is colourful and bright,

Where the sun shines all day and the moon shines all night,
I wish we could live in a time like this.

Arielle Amelia Danaie-Agate (13)
Hove Park School, Hove

Am I The Only One?

Am I the only one who misses being a kid?
Dancing in the rain like tomorrow was just a day,
Waking up each morning and being excited by what awaits,
Seeing friends and laughing, not knowing the meaning of
loss,
Going to sleep and not dreading waking up,
Dreaming all sorts of futures like anything is possible,
Crushing on people and not knowing what pain love brings,
Being able to laugh tears away and hate being just a word,
Being innocent and not knowing the world's dangers,
Not knowing the dangers of being a woman,
Not knowing the dangers of being black,
Not knowing the dangers of being gay,
Not knowing pain, fear, war,
Not knowing what it's like to lose someone you love,
Not knowing that one difference or flaw you possess
Society will use to drag you down,
But this is the world we have created for the future kids,
People killing others without reasoning,
People being segregated for the way they look,
People being bullied to the point of breaking,
People, just horrible people,
Why has society done this to people?
Am I the only one that thinks we need to change?

Emily Sweeney Bruce (14)
Hove Park School, Hove

35

Me

I am young,
I am small,
I am strong,
I am creative,
I am clever,
I am healthy,
I am unique,
I am a girl,
I am.

To be fair,
To not care,
Let them think,
Don't even blink,
You do your thing,
They do their thing,
They can be mean,
Make things clean,
End it,
Don't read too much into it,
Jealous,
Upset,
Wanting to be your friend.

Be yourself,
Himself,
Herself,

Why does it matter?
Don't be a tagger,
All alone,
Tell someone.

You are you,
You don't have to,
Don't listen,
You're your own division.

Don't change for them,
Don't run for them,
Don't risk for them.

They will hurt you,
Out of the blue,
There's few,
Who like you for you!

Help, stand up today,
Don't wait in the bay,
Go help and play.

Put your hair up in a bun,
Don't be outdone,
Find your one,
Don't run,
Get everyone and
Have fun.

If you see unkindness,
Go over to them,
Give them a yes!

Xanthe Cox (12)
Hove Park School, Hove

Plastic And Wildlife

P eople use plastic in their lives every day,
L eaving litter in wildlife where creatures must stay,
A nimals suffer, many lives can end,
S uffocating on plastic is too harmful to mend.
T urtles choke on plastic while hunting for food,
I n one simple action, that plastic wouldn't be chewed.
C reatures get trapped in nets and eat bottle tops.

A nyone could change this but it just never stops,
N atural habitats are destroyed because of our waste,
D umping plastic leaves many animals displaced.

W hen seals are swimming, they get caught in our litter,
I f we were less thoughtless, their endings wouldn't be so bitter.
L ittle things like bottle lids can end an innocent life,
D ucks are strangled by soda holders, plastic acts like a knife,
L ots of animals are injured by plastic each year,
I t harms creatures, like seabirds and otters and deer
F atal injuries are caused by waste in the wild and zoos,
E veryone can change this so why shouldn't you?

Rosabelle Jones (11)
Hove Park School, Hove

Words

Words have the power to do great things,
But very often, they abuse that power,
This power often makes petty humans cower,
Words have power above every other thing.

The power of words is strong,
It can do good, it can do wrong,
Words can destroy someone, they can fill them with glee,
Words can give happiness, they can make them run away and flee,
They can wreck your hopes, onto them you cling,
Words have power above every other thing.

Words have the power to do great things,
But very often, they abuse that power,
This power often makes petty humans cower,
Words have power above every other thing.

They can manipulate people, they can influence people,
They can cut through you like a knife through butter,
Death is their favourite word, this they often mutter,
They can haunt and they can taunt,
Words can make someone cry, they can make someone sing,
Words have power above every other thing.

Words have the power to do great things,
But very often, they abuse that power,

This power often makes petty humans cower,
Words have power above every other thing.

Solly Al-Hussaini (11)
Hove Park School, Hove

Holocaust Shock

The gas chambers, the crowding, the upset and the shock
When your head was thrown on the chopping block
I may not mean that literally
And maybe it is true
But one thing I know for certain
Is that it wouldn't be nice if that were you
Steven is distraught
Steven is broken
Steven has fought
But he has been shaken
And as he said
I have no more room for hatred
Steven is Dutch
Steven is proud
Steven has as much
Pride and happiness
As you
To his mum, dad, uncle and aunt
To the brave souls that died and can't
Be here to see
And live their own story
Not the one that Hitler told
But the ones of the brave and the bold
Not the ones that sell for gold
But the ones of the young and old
Steven was seven

Steven was upset
Steven can't be even
Steven will never forget
The treachery of his youth
But here is proof
That people can live without
Dwelling about
The anger inside of them
And stop it from getting out
Steven can live in peace
Has no anger
Steven has no beast
Steven is happier
You should be too.

Rowan Eckworth-Jones (11)
Hove Park School, Hove

Enemy Or Ally?

War, war,
It's just like before,
The fire calls for more and for more,
'Til it shakes us to the core,
But what? But what is this tragedy for?

When it starts, it never ends,
Who's the villain? Who's the friend?
'Friends' always come and pretend,
Then the hate messages send and send.

When the kids look, they say they envy,
But we got problems, we got plenty.

They think we fuss about homework,
But the actual reality drives us berserk,
Bullies are the predators that lurk,
They trick and fill our eyes with murk.

I don't know who to trust,
I don't know who to hurt.

Enemy or ally, who is who?
Love or like? I don't know what to choose,
It's not like any can be used,
But the more we hate, the more we abuse.

As you can see, it's more than you think,
The madness we experience takes us to the brink.

The more we feel pain, the more we want to sink,
Let's see if you can find the link.

In the adult world, there are many wars,
But in school, we have our own to fight for.

Silver Mira Evans (11)
Hove Park School, Hove

Dear Earth

Dear Earth,
Look around you, what do you see?
Factories instead of trees,
Waste under the seas,
Is this how you want to be treated?
You are being destroyed,
How are you not severely annoyed?

Smoke instead of oxygen,
Power plants and tall buildings,
What about the fields, meadows and everything in-
between?
No one thinks about them.

Why do you let society do this to you?
Why, oh why, do you not fire back?
Or decide to end it all?
What about wildlife?
What about nature?
Defend yourself Earth, why hold back?

You must feel so cheated,
You must feel so depressed,
Tell us how you feel in any way you can express,
You must be so afraid,
Afraid that maybe something could cause you to leave this
universe,

Afraid that something could attack you,
Afraid of the future,
I know how you feel.

Why do you still keep society alive
When we harm you every day?
Why do you still keep us safe
When we treat you this way?
Dear Earth, I hope you understand
Some of us still care about you
And want to give you a helping hand.

Helen Martin (12)
Hove Park School, Hove

I Wonder...

Swimming for their lives,
Half-dead,
Losing the will to live.

A mother clinging to her child,
Nowhere to rest,
She had to keep going.

It didn't matter that she
Was soaked to the skin,
It didn't matter that her eyes
Were so full of water she could barely see,
It didn't matter that her
Muscles were frozen from lack of sleep and cold,
It only mattered that she kept going
And kept her child alive.

Hope,
A spark,
A flame,
An explosion.

Gunshots pierced the air,
Another attack,
No one was safe,
Nowhere was safe.

Living in a terrorist country,

Had never been this bad before,
But now,
With his mother and father dead,
He wanted to leave,
To escape,
To be somewhere else,
Anywhere else,
Just not here.

They were back,
Back again to outnumber and abuse him,
Back again to taunt and torment him,
Back again to make his life a living hell,
He wished they would leave him alone.

Katie Harrison (12)
Hove Park School, Hove

Plastic In The Sea

Plastic, I just don't understand,
Why people throw it in the sea and the sand,
Beautiful seas and sapphire oceans,
But all of a sudden, there has been a plastic explosion,
Plastic in the water, killing sea creatures big and small,
Soon, there will be nothing to see at all,
Swimmers and deep-sea divers will have only one big wish,
To see no plastic and rubbish, instead, amazing, colourful fish,
A beautiful world with clear seas is what we need,
Not mountains of rubbish to stop the animals breed.

It's not that hard to throw your rubbish in the bin,
Otherwise, people in the future won't be able to see the sea creatures swim,
There is too much plastic in the sea,
Dumped there by people like you and me,
Dolphins, fish and little seals
Are starting to think that plastic is their meal,
Plastic is everywhere, in shops, houses and schools,
But plastic in the sea is not cool,
So stop destroying the seas and creatures because it's cruel,
This is now the most important rule.

Chloe Smith (12)
Hove Park School, Hove

PTSD

Alone, every night haunted
Battlefield, out there every day, fighting
Capture the enemy, they have family too
Death, friends lifeless everywhere
Enemy, must kill, must attack
Fear, fear of death, fear of life
Government, controlling, watching
Harsh conditions, harsh life
Impact, never recover
Join, must fight, must not worry, be a man!
Kill the enemy
Loyalty, fight for the country
Massacre, must kill everyone from the other side
Nightmare every night
Officials, watching, controlling
Propaganda telling us to fight, to become a 'happy warrior'
Quest, must complete
Recover, will never happen
Struggle, struggle, struggle daily
Trenches, deep, dirty
Unhealthy, physically, mentally
Vanish, missing, *poof*, gone!
War, never again
Yelling loud, death
Zone, in the zone.

Ciara Denyer (13)
Hove Park School, Hove

Like A Girl

I'm on the field with my team behind me,
The balls on the floor and I give it a whirl,
I miss.
"You kick like a girl!"

I'm on the track with my foes behind me,
The race begins and I run with a hurl,
Second.
"You run like a girl!"

I'm in the pool with my opponents behind me,
The competition starts in the water pearl,
Beaten.
"You swim like a girl!"

I'm on the stage with the crowd behind me,
The judges call and I begin with a twirl,
I fall.
"You dance like a girl!"

Why should 'like a girl' be an insult?
Why should it discourage young girls and boys?
Why should it be used every single day?
Why should I get Barbies and they get dumper truck toys?

But I wake up 'like a girl',
I sleep 'like a girl',
I eat 'like a girl',

I learn 'like a girl',
Because I am a girl!
And I'm proud to be a girl.

Katie Galloway (12)
Hove Park School, Hove

World Of Peace

In war, there are no victors,
No champions, no heroes,
Just the side of the last man standing,
The side that doth remain.

Hardships outweigh the spoils,
Regret and full of shame,
To see another's face before they die,
A never-ending pain.

Loved ones worst affected,
Tormented day and night,
The world would be in better shape,
If the world could cease its fight.

Seemingly impossible,
To reach the utopian goal,
Yet if we keep on trying,
We shall beat this foe.

Our quarrels can be sorted,
Our differences accepted,
Our fighting finally over,
Peace long-lasting, no more bloodshed.

This is the perfect world,
A world within our reach,

Humans are the answer,
To an everlasting peace.

Jake Rees (14)
Hove Park School, Hove

Happiness

Happy is when you feel good about who you are,
Happy is when you aren't afraid to shoot for the stars,
What is happiness? they say.

Happiness is when you face reality
Happiness is when you make your fantasy
Happiness is when you aren't scared of tragedy
What is sadness? they say.

Sadness is when you get out of bed in sorrow
Sadness is when you are demonising tomorrow
What is sadness? they say.

Sadness is when doors are all locked
Sadness is when all hope is lost
Sadness is when ambition is tossed.

You've only got two choices
Camouflage your feelings and regret it today
Or
You get up and confront them and be grateful the next day.

You never heal instantly
But never regret trying to do so.

Nafisa Sofian Miah (13)
Hove Park School, Hove

Sour Thoughts

These thoughts inside my head cramp up,
Lead me down streets and such,
Alleyways I didn't think I had,
Things that want to make me sad,
Block them out with laughter and jokes,
I'll call these thoughts a total hoax,
These little things maybe do matter,
But I always seem to choose the latter.

They'll poke me, choke me,
Do whatever they can to provoke me,
Things like: "Oh, you're such a horrible person."
Maybe nip it in the bud before it can worsen,
People only laugh at your jokes for pity's sake,
When in actual fact, you give them a headache,
Does everyone have these thoughts?
Stop trying to pretend you're anything from the norm!

Nancy Hazel Pixie Hinde (12)
Hove Park School, Hove

Guns In America

People are suffering
Can't you see
That you don't need guns
To have fun?
You don't need guns
To protect yourself
Because strong people fight with their words
Not their fists
Just put the guns down
Don't be a clown
Can't you understand
That you don't need guns
To be safe?
There's just so much hate
In 2015
There were 33,636 deaths
I just want you to know
That guns should be banned
Because people are dying
Look at Florida
It was the deadliest shooting
17 people were killed
What about the families
Who lost their children?
They must be devastated
So now you know

How important it is
Please, just listen to this.

Betsy Davies (11)
Hove Park School, Hove

Mother, They Have Guns

Knock knock! "Open up!
We are not here to rob,
Just to get in touch."

Through the peephole, I looked,
"Mother, they have guns,
The big ones that shoot a ton!"

Under the bed, into the bathroom,
We filled all the hiding places but they found us,
Found us, took us, tortured us.

I woke up,
"Where am I?
Mother, Brother, are you anywhere nearby?
What's going to happen? Are we going to die?"

Years have passed now, still getting by,
Parents risk their lives just to keep us alive.

If you read this, know it was torture,
Please don't let this happen again in the future.

Illango Kata Bogschutz (12)
Hove Park School, Hove

I Am A Jew

I am a Jew
I am forced to wear a dull gold star
And if I could, I would have left my unforgettable scar.

I am a Jew
I don't know where they are taking me
But they have taken all my things so when I get there
Everything must be free.

Days have gone by
More than one has said goodbye
But I, not yet, will admit to my lies.

I don't know what I have done
Nor do I remember where I am from
And all my hopes of escape were gone within a day.

I don't know my name
I don't know my age
I just know I'm locked up in a cage
All skinny and thin
I wonder how much Hitler has thrown into the bin.

Charlotte Devriendt (11)
Hove Park School, Hove

Our Stars

In the dark, empty night sky
Stars fill this darkness, a hollow space
And yet they still sparkle ever so brightly...
Yet soon fade away in the blazing light of the sun
The once pitch-black sky turns piercing blue...
As you wish your hopes and dreams on the stars
As the forever-moving clouds pass you by
The stars in the night sky stay unmoving and never pass you by
As for you are the moon, lighting the way in the darkness
The stars are your hopes, dreams, wishes and everything you hold dearly
While the sun is taking your stars away from you
And replacing them with clouds...
Don't let it take your stars...
No one should take your stars.

Ruby Michelle Hopkins (13)
Hove Park School, Hove

The Weeping Woman

The weeping woman weeping away
Looking so sad and glum
With dysfunctional shapes all over her face!

The weeping woman with a lovely flower
On her magnificent, red summer hat
With an outstanding yellow and pink dress
That stands out of the crowd.

The weeping woman's hair is like thousands of fluffy blankets
One on top of another on top of a treetop
With millions of roses falling off the branches onto her flower hat!

The weeping woman has a very nice appearance
But there's one thing from stopping her happiness
Sadly, she's waiting
Waiting for something to be done about her anxiety!

Myani-Brooke Hawsdon-Healy (11)
Hove Park School, Hove

Am I Good Enough?

Writing all these poems, thinking they are not good enough
Trying to express my pain but yet, my pain is not good enough
Trying to tell you about the dark figure that follows me everywhere
Trying to tell you I don't belong in this Muggle world but do belong at Hogwarts
Trying to tell you I am not strong enough for this
But yet, it's not good enough
When we were young, we didn't worry about what was good enough
And had no care for other's opinions, but we grew up to
Now I hide my body in fear and throw away my art in shame
Yet, I am good enough, you just try to hide that from me!

Abigail Jeffery (13)
Hove Park School, Hove

Cliché

Girls with short skirts and silky hair
Are known to be popular
Athletic boys with golden hair
Are known to be stronger
Black girls with weaves and braids
Are known as ghetto
Smart boys with glasses
Are seen as a geek to most
A Muslim girl with a hijab
Is automatically classified as a terrorist
Poets are known to be boring
As they fight with words and not with their fists
However, we're much more than that
And that's what people cannot see
They're blinded by our greatness
And overpowered by jealousy
That's the world's greatest enemy.

Haddy Loum (12)
Hove Park School, Hove

Cliché

Girls with short skirts and silky hair
Are known to be popular
Athletic boys with golden hair
Are known to be stronger
Black girls with weaves and braids
Are known as ghetto
Smart boys with glasses
Are seen as a geek to most
A Muslim girl with a hijab
Is automatically classified as a terrorist
Poets are known to be boring
As they fight with words and not with their fists
However, we're much more than that
And that's what people cannot see
They're blinded by our greatness
And overpowered by jealousy
That's the world's greatest enemy.

Toumma Touray (11)
Hove Park School, Hove

Now Gone!

I see torn-down buildings,
Abandoned, bleak, solitary,
Citizens' homes,
Now gone.
I see army trucks,
Decreasing in size,
Edging towards the horizon,
Soldiers' targets,
Now gone.

I see silent, mournful children
Eager for food,
Forlorn, dismal, isolated,
Meal times filled with family laughter,
Now gone.
I see an armless teddy bear,
Blanketed by rubble,
A distant memory of comfort,
The soul of home,
Now gone.

My eyes are a mirror of suffering,
My eyes echo anguish,
My eyes are a reflection of war.

Macy Brooking (11)
Hove Park School, Hove

Aren't Labels Just For Food?

Boys have Action Men
And play with small guns
They also play football
And boys have fun.

Girls like cooking
And they look cute
They also play with dolls
And definitely can't shoot.

Boys get their clothes muddy
Their hair is cut short
They also play the drums
And have always fought.

Girls wear make-up
And go on diets
They are also graceful
And girls are quiet.

What is the point in these labels?
These labels which define your gender
Aren't labels just for food?

Maisie Barrett (11)
Hove Park School, Hove

What Is The World Coming To?

What is the world coming to?
With global warming every day,
"Cut down on electronics,"
Our teachers all say.

What is the world coming to?
With penguins on thin ice,
We look around and think,
Well, that's not very nice.

What is the world coming to?
With trafficking and war,
I thought we abolished that
Many years before.

But we don't do a thing,
Not one thing at all,
And we all have to change that
Or the world will fall.

What is the world coming to?

Fintan Crean (12)
Hove Park School, Hove

Hunted

We were in a sanctuary,
Living life at ease,
But the moment night fell,
Something whispered through the trees.

Voices as calm as guns,
Echoed through the night
And tears blurred my vision,
As I huddled up tight.

I closed my eyes and tried to remember,
The world I never thought I'd leave,
I wonder if there will ever be,
A place I feel so warm to perceive.

How could these things happen?
How could we lose so much?
From just a few bad people
And one cruel blade's touch...

Leelah Affleck (12)
Hove Park School, Hove

Treasured Friends!

You deserve somebody who fits you like a glove,
Crazy, mad and passionate love,
You deserve somebody who makes your soul glow,
Who takes the time to find out all there is to know,
Sincere individual, perfect joy,
Making you feel as excited as a little girl or boy,
Companionship and true loyalty
With a friendship that is as comfortable as can be,
They make you feel safe so your heart can open,
Trust given, fear broken,
Love can be experienced, shared or alone,
The love you are given will be the greatest ever known!

Jasmine Butler (12)
Hove Park School, Hove

The Bloody War

Running around the trenches,
The taste of blood running around my jaw,
Sitting lonely in the benches,
This is the life of war.

The taste of gas dribbling around my tongue,
My life is so miserable,
I can feel it in my lungs,
My pain is so deep, it's even visible.

Life is so deep,
The feeling I can feel,
The advantages I can't reach,
The war is so real.

I'm sitting in the trenches
The feeling is so raw,
Last thing to say,
This is the bloody war.

Ilias Boughelam (13)
Hove Park School, Hove

Volar (Fly)

You're gone
Where?
Where the light shone
You've gone
Where the light shines
You've left.

I'm alone again
I'm alone with my thoughts
The image distorts
I'm lost again
I'm trapped again.

I conjure you up
For a moment, I'm calm
My breathing slow
Sweat on my palm.

For a second, you're there
Keeping me sane
Then you're gone again.

If I could fly as a bird flies
I would be close to you.

Matilda Waterman (12)
Hove Park School, Hove

If I Could Wish

If I could wish, I would wish that the world would not be so greedy
If I could wish, I would wish that there would be no homeless people
If I could wish, I would wish that no one would harm one another
If I could wish, I would wish that everyone would live in peace and harmony
If I could wish, I would wish that everyone would be created equal
If I could wish, I would wish that there would be no pollution in the world
If I could wish, the world would be a better place.

Helayna Fern (11)
Hove Park School, Hove

Boom!

I was in my room
Then I heard a loud *boom!*
I didn't know what was going on
So I turned the light on
Then I jumped out of bed
And woke up my brother, Ted
And we wanted to investigate the boom
So we ran out of the room
We paced downstairs
And sat down in our pair
And tried to think of what it was.

Then we heard it again...

Then we saw it was our cat
Jumping off the sofa, onto the doormat.

Kaja Stepien (11)
Hove Park School, Hove

The Bare Minimum

Never try the bare minimum,
Always your best,
Every job you can think of,
From a footballer to a vet!

Never try the bare minimum,
Always your best,
To play in the biggest countries,
In the biggest stadium,
For the biggest team.
You have to train hard and eat healthier,
If you want to be wealthier.

Nothing ever is a chance,
You have to take risks,
Never try the bare minimum,
Always your best.

Joel Crute (12)
Hove Park School, Hove

Searching

Down on his knees
Tears flow from restless tired eyes
Drool drips from his blood-splattered uniform
His feet run cold.

Thoughts of pain and suffering meander through his
desperate mind
When will this hell be over?
Searching for the lives of his friends like birds of prey
What he doesn't realise is that he is the prey.

He won't give up, not now, not ever!

When will this wicked war end?

Heli Cook (12)
Hove Park School, Hove

The Forest

Rabbit, deer, robin, mouse
Use the forest as a house
Beauty, splendour all around
It exists, even underground
Pools of water full of fish
Swimming about as they wish
Then the humans butchered all
And killed all those who opposed their rule
Dread began to spread its wings
And envelope every living thing
Creatures now know humans as satanic
As their greed and hatred will destroy the planet.

Llewellyn Curtis (14)
Hove Park School, Hove

Brexit

Brexit
Why exit?
Why did it get voted for?
They said more power
It's actually more stress
It's all a mess
Fake news
Gets views
Let's choose
To stop
To mop away
Theresa May
What's wrong with the EU?
You choose
The NHS was promised millions
Sounded brilliant
But where's the cash?
More like a crash!
The country is going to die
Why?

Dylan Barker (11)
Hove Park School, Hove

Racism

Racism, racism
What does it matter
If we're not all the same colour?

Some of us are black
Some of us are white
But we are all alright.

So don't do it
Don't be mean about races
Because it doesn't matter about faces.

We are all the same
So don't have shame
Be proud of who you are
Because you are a star.

Nuha Choudhury (12)
Hove Park School, Hove

Knife Crime

People are suffering
People are recovering.

The world's not safe
You have to escape.

There's so much hate
You'll reach your fate.

Millions die every second
You could be threatened.

Knives are dangerous
You have to be courageous.

Stop killing
Valuable lives.

Sharna Dooley (12)
Hove Park School, Hove

Brighton

In Brighton, seagulls roam,
I watch them from my window at home,
On Brighton Pier, there are lots of rides,
We ride the bumper cars, they always collide.
In Brighton, there are lots of shops,
And Churchill Square is at the top.
When I'm on the i360,
I feel like I'll fall and become history!

Felix Pearcey (11)
Hove Park School, Hove

The Sea Guard

The ocean sea splashes
Against the wall
Of my garden gate
My gate will close
When my brain goes
And the waves will
Fall to the ground.

Biba Loosemore (12)
Hove Park School, Hove

Buried Alive

I'm in a wooden box under the ground,
The dirt above me weighing me down,
It's dead quiet as I lay,
Wondering if it's night or day,
Can anyone hear me screaming and shouting?
But I am most definitely doubting,
Millions of questions fly through my mind,
But the darkness surrounds me and makes me feel blind,
Can anyone hear me? I'm all alone
And I feel so empty, with pain in every bone,
As I'm in a wooden box under the ground,
The dirt above me weighing me down.

I'm in a wooden box under the ground,
The dirt above me weighing me down,
I try not to panic but I begin to pray
And I say, "Hey, I want to get out, okay?"
I look for every possible way out
And every corner, no doubt!
I can't breathe! I'm running out of air,
So I try not to speak, which is extremely rare.
I miss my family and the beaming sun
And playing with my kids, which I find really fun,
But I'm in a wooden box under the ground,
The dirt above me is weighing me down.

I'm in a wooden box under the ground,

The dirt above me is weighing me down,
I miss the drumming sound of rain against the window
And the fluffy clouds in the blissful, blue sky drifting so slow
And the luxury of a duvet in a snuggly, warm place
And where all my dreams were of me being safe,
But I'm in a wooden box under the ground,
The dirt above me is weighing me down.

Hannah Irving (13)
Maplesden Noakes School, Great Buckland

Fantasize (Mind World)

Just picture a world with no expression,
No welcoming and pure grin to embrace you at the station
And no enlivening laugh when you share experiences,
We just cannot understand the bubbly gaze or the innocent
glance when we helplessly fall in love,
We're nothing but lifeless and lonely carriages rolling
nonchalantly across precarious tracks
And only words can justify why I was so separated from
sensibility that day.

Just illustrate a cease of interest,
No extensive expeditions to uncover unnoticed,
No tuning into our ever-shifting heavens night and day,
We can no longer recall why we adopted the decision to
plummet into admiration,
Yet, you are anything but affected by me, for I am just a
moth, hopelessly drawn to a flame
And only fabricated portraits could ever fasten a ribbon
between mine and your nature.

Just envision this world lacking contact,
No events to furnish your soul with fresh desires of others,
No skill to unearth your own peculiarity,
We are no longer adequate to display and demonstrate our
own talents to our own families,
We cannot read an exhilarating book and let the creatures
become more than figures of the mind
And it is now we set aside this imaginary world and see how
incredible ours is.

Esther Gardner (13)

Maplesden Noakes School, Great Buckland

The Life Sentence

A deathly silence filled the air
As the only thing that was heard
Was the harsh clicking of the guards' heels
Approaching the cell.

The uniformed Reapers looked down
On the ghostly bundle of apprehension.

Thrust around like leaves in the wind
The disinclined jailbird wanted
To stay behind the bars
That never used to feel like home.

Pushing, pulling, round and round,
Up and down - why now?
Breathing, panting, what have I done?
An eye for an eye, I know
But where am I going to go
When I am as white as snow?

I get it, I regret it, my lesson is learned
I'll be six feet under, no time to wonder
Choking - I splutter, my life?
Not a mutter.

Charlotte Rickard (14)
Maplesden Noakes School, Great Buckland

Free

With every long step forward I take,
A protective wall inside of me will break,
Although you may say, "Oh, she's only fourteen,"
Life for me isn't as easy as it seems.

All the scars I've managed to hide away,
Someone else has had to pay,
For my stupid mistakes have cost my friends
And will continue until the very end.

I have a whole new life ahead of me,
But no one seems to want to spend it with me,
No one says 'we' or 'us' or 'together',
They shove me down until I lose my tether.

I slave away, doing homework and school work,
Always trying to find that innocent perk,
But it's just not there,
Again, I sit here crying in despair.

One comment, one word could make me shatter,
They don't bother to ask whatever's the matter,
Why don't you understand?
Why are people so ignorant in this land?

Give someone the hope that they deserve,
Go on, just do it, I know you have the nerve.

Spare them their life, their arm or wrist,
Give them a hug, a kiss that they've missed.

Meredith King (14)
Maplesden Noakes School, Great Buckland

Transgender

The reflection which haunted her, the image which frightened him,
The self-pain that hit her, the wounds that were upon him.

As she cried, it became a blur; as he cut, it became a sin,
As the day rose, it punished her; as the night fell, it scarred him.

Society told her to look nice,
Society told him to defend,
Society made things so precise,
Society broke what may not mend.

She fell to the floor, he fell on the bed,
She just couldn't take it anymore,
All those words roaming in his head.

Laws aren't the same,
Our lives have their own lanes,
Yet, people are afraid to change how they were made.

People have their own views, but to discriminate is to lose
No one should end up in a hearse because they were pushed to the very worst.

He finally wore shorts with no top on the basketball courts,
She dressed like a queen, showing her curves like a beauty machine.

The reflection he knew, the image she welcomed,
The self-pain he blocked, the wounds she forgot.

April Shanahan (13)
Maplesden Noakes School, Great Buckland

It's My Job

I'm not a stranger to the dark,
I'm pure evil,
Shaped like death,
I've got a golden point to kill,
A murky army surrounding me,
Men's cries fill me with delight,
Another man's job well done,
My job takes all day,
All night,
Every day,
For years.

Those men's lives hiding in the treacherous trenches,
Not worth a second of that time,
For now, they all die,
My friends race to see,
Who will kill the innocent first?
I've watched hundreds of hearts burst,
It pleases me knowing thousands came,
But only a few hundred have left,
Even then, my murky army has injured them.

Cries for help come from all around,
Then one by one,
Men hit the ground,
The thundering sound of an angry storm,
Changes the atmosphere like a light switch on the wall,

There is no safeness in this death zone,
No walls keeping us enclosed,
Yet, no reconcile,
No retreat.

Libby Rogers (12)
Maplesden Noakes School, Great Buckland

The Depths Of My Despair

Burnt-out lights are all I see
And with it comes the silence,
My thoughts are drab and debris,
I can't stand in defiance.
It suffocates me day by day,
As my last words try to stay,
My lonely mind has turned to grey,
All that is left has wasted away.

The dark thoughts that crowd my mind,
A lot of confidence is lost
And it leaves me wary to find,
Where who I truly am was tossed.
Monsters live under my bed,
They follow me everywhere,
The darkness that lives in my head
Always makes people stop and stare.

Remorse that seeps through my skin,
The worry that paints my face,
Pain that's in my eyes,
Trouble in every breath.
They've held me captive for so long,
My mask of joy is starting to wear,
My friends ask me what's wrong,

They've noticed the small rips and tears.

I'm fine.

Isobel Browning (13)
Maplesden Noakes School, Great Buckland

Escape

Water splashes against my face,
All I can see is a disgrace,
The mirror doesn't lie,
When I see - in my eye -
The red of my blood
Creating a flood
Of memories I never wished to see,
Shake my head to be free -
But I relive the gunfire,
The barbed wire,
My hands shake
And my legs quake,
The world turns
Deeper and deeper still,
I remember his eyes would spill
The colours of crimson
That blurred his vision,
Looking down,
I almost drown
In the memory of my hands and fingers,
That were covered in blood - which still lingers.
My heart beats quicker
And in a flicker,
The world stops -
My stomach drops,
A past I wish to forget

Has me dripping in sweat,
In the mirror, there I stand,
Blood still dripping from my hand.

Holly Irving (16)
Maplesden Noakes School, Great Buckland

Pressure

Beep! Beep!

Pressure, worry, fear.

Join Instagram
Don't post that
Ugly, fat, nobody.

Pressure, worry, fear.

Join Snapchat, use a filter
Not so ugly
Ashamed, changed, hidden.

Pressure, worry, fear.

Too much, too much pressure
Panic, anxiety, depression
Help, can't breathe
Show something, make-up on, short skirt
So fat, must lose weight
Stop!

I'm not ugly, I'm beautiful
Breathe
I can be who I want to be
Show what I want to show
Live my life
No pressure.

Francesca Thomas (15)
Maplesden Noakes School, Great Buckland

Emmett Till

The news has spread,
A black boy dead,
A simple lie
Caused the boy to die!

Gouged and gory,
Only Emmett knows the story,
Bullet in the head, caved-in eye,
Mum's in bits and forced to sigh!

This is murder, are you dumb?
As innocent Emmett Till only wanted gum,
Chicago was his hometown
And all the locals are left to frown!

"Ah, wolf whistle, attack, attack!"
Little Till got beaten up by the pack,
Kidnapped and full of shiver,
As now dead Emmett is found in a river!

Harry Spain (14)
Maplesden Noakes School, Great Buckland

The Reaper's Calling

In his glass cage, he lies
Looking strong with pride,
Where he puts down his arms to die,
But only lived for the ride.

Everyone dances with the Grim Reaper,
Just a matter of time,
With nothing any deeper
Rugged with the crime.

Whimpering sighs from the demons inside,
Crawling and crying from the brain,
Miming, *I'll be alright.*

Alexander Coulton (14)
Maplesden Noakes School, Great Buckland

I'll Beware

Hello, hello, is anyone there?
I feel so small,
Won't someone care?
I'm not allowed to call -
How could I be such a fool?

It's so cold
And I'm all alone,
I just wish I had the strength to be bold,
But instead, I'm here, shaken to the bone,
As I'm being controlled.

They call the shots,
Whilst I'm kept here against my will,
Hands shake as I tie the knots,
I think, *how many more will they steal?*

Yet, as I stand here, against the world,
I break free of my restraints,
Break free of this nightmare:
I need to tell them they won't control my fate.

Stepping down, I break loose of the chains.
I realise there never was a truce
Because you are my depression
And I will beware.

Adrian Simmons (15)
Robert Clack School, Dagenham

It's No Longer Small

Death plays my music
I sit front row of that symphony.

The voices inside my head
Keep playing on repeat
I scream, they just never seem
To leave me.

I am too blind to see,
Everything that I could be.
Let my life shatter,
Does it even matter?
Letting the truth sink in,
Peace in my mind is not for me,
My life means as much to me
As the rung-out teabag used for Nan's tea.

Opening up was a moment
Far from my proudest,
Words always are stuck,
Even when I am shouting my loudest.

It is my fight to fight,
My battle to face,
I thought I could conquer the nights alone,
Yet, that isn't the case.

My feelings and thoughts have never gone away,

I'm sorry that I think I'm not meant to stay.

Everything I am,
I'm not trying to be,
I don't mean to seem sad
I need to, you see.

You have better days ahead of you
I just pray you do see,
Please,
Please, just listen to me.

You were created for more
Than to die in this place,
I need to throw it,
Just throw your depression away.

Away as well as the tear-stained face,
The ones that have smiles all over the place.

Some people believe the lies
That it's best to die,
They think it's the simple way out but,
Think about it,
They never got to see how it all turned out.

It may just be your messed-up fate,
But save yourself before it's too late.

They ask me how I am,
I say I'm always fine

As I look down at my arms
At those old, white lines.

The time I gave up,
The time it took over,
It just wasn't a dream,
But thankfully, it wasn't my goodbye either.

Inside, your insecurities are dying to bust out,
You cut your friends off,
So you've got nobody now,
You need help and you know,
But you can't be another one of those 'freak shows'.

I hear the same each time,
It's like depression is a crime,
'It's all in your head',
'Be happy',
'Happiness is a choice',
If it were a choice,
Then why can't I be happy?
Why am I numb?

Not even sad?
Tell me, do you think I'm mad?

Tell me, tell me now!

You tell us to speak up,
But when we do, we are ignored,

Pushed away,
Not given a say,
We keep it bottled,
Feelings locked in the drawer,
Key thrown away,
Never to be seen again.

And when we blew,
You say you never knew
Even though we pleaded,
Pleaded to you,
Pleaded for support,
Pleaded for help,
What did we get in return?
The disappointment you felt,
That, that was always your 'help'.

Why, why?
Please tell me now,
Will my children live like this?
Their thoughts
All dismissed,
The silver blades,
Then red skies,
Their minds going to thoughts,
My children wanting to die!
Is that what awaits?
Awaits them soon,

In a world where flowers
Might not even bloom.

Tell me, tell me now!

Is this what society wants from me?
For me to break down?
Share it all
We can't live like this anymore,
It's no longer 'small'.

Yasmin Cabak (14)
Robert Clack School Of Science, Dagenham

Society Today

We are defined by the colour of our skin
And not by the purity of our hearts,
Smiles being taken for granted every day,
Frowns being turned into tears in every possible way.

This society we are classed in today
Really drives young people astray,
Drugs, rapes and murders worst of all,
Really causes thunders of waterfalls,
Because sometimes I really pray to God that he comes,
saves and heals all.

Spending ages in the mirror because we know we'll get
judged for how we look,
Always trying to look good for the schoolbook,
But no matter how hard we try, our faces get talked about
more than the talkbook
Because this is the society we live in today.

Society isn't us, we are society,
We define society, it doesn't define us,
So let's make a change and not put this up to discuss.

Because the society we live in today
Is full of fear, violence, hate and inequality
So we have to make a change! We just have to
Because maybe, who knows, together we can make a
breakthrough.

Jaynell Prempeh (13)
Robert Clack School Of Science, Dagenham

Our Voices

"You're a child," they say
"You don't know the world that well."
And you're right, it's true
We get it - I'm not as old as you
But does that still mean we have to be silenced?
That our voices have to stay quiet sirens?
'Cause that's the thing
You act like there's nothing for us to be stating
But really, the sirens inside us are blaring
Our minds are younger
We see things that you would probably look over
And if you just let us open our mouths
You might be able to see things the way we do
You might just realise that our voices matter too.

We see our friends - the ones distraught with pain
How they cut scars deep into their veins
And we know how we look at God and we cry and pray
Telling him to show our friends the light of day
'Cause that's the thing
We know how bad the words can hurt
So your bones are broken until they're dust
But what if we had done something?
If the kids who saw had spoken out before?
If only we had a platform to tell them their beauty glows...

And we know the kids that come into school looking tired

How really their brains are totally fired
Fired with drugs that course through their body
How the perfume can't mask the reeking of weed and
ecstasy
'Cause that's the thing
You only see their bad decision
But do you know the peer pressure they were given?
But now they sit in a whirlwind mist of poison
Lost in their web of addiction
But what if we had done something?
If the kids who saw had spoken out before?
If only we had a platform to tell them drugs put their minds
at war...

And don't forget the class troublemakers sent out of lesson
every day
They always seem to leave with giggles waving them away
You ever wondered why?
Maybe their protests had been laced with truth
Maybe they really were only bearing good fruit
You saw something amiss - so you quickly signed your
verdict against them
But you were wrong - you'd blindly blamed based on
previous seasons
'Cause that's the thing
People change! You always tell us to
But you never believe us when we finally do
But what if we had done something?

If the kids who saw had spoken out before?
If only we had a platform to say we really had mended our flaws...

You're right, we are just children
Our minds are young and
Our voices are sirens -
We're not meant to be silenced.
Sirens are loud and blaring
And when they sound, they should be taken as warnings
'Cause that's the thing
Our sirens could be forces of help
And if they were trained correctly,
The red of our sirens wouldn't mean anger
It would mean
Love.

Persis George (14)
Robert Clack School Of Science, Dagenham

Expectations

Having to live up to expectations
People having to live up to expectations, no matter who
they are
Some have high expectations, others have low.

Families wanting their children to set their sights higher
Parents having expectations to set an example for their
child
In order for them to be in a high-paying job.

Some students feeling the pressure is rising to do well in
their exams
As it makes or breaks the foundation for their future
Wanting to do well to get a profitable job
To accumulate a fortune for future generations to live
comfortable
Without needing to work as vigorously as their predecessor.

Some treated like outcasts because they cannot live up to
expectations
But all a person needs to do to overcome the fear of not
making expected progress
Is not to focus on what is to be expected
But to focus on the very thing that they are doing and
should do
With all the strength that they can muster and move on
forward.

Jackie Bukari (14)
Robert Clack School Of Science, Dagenham

Online Poison

You people behind your screens
The ones who shout online
Poison the waters of threads
Hurt those with opinions different from mine.

Why do you feel it's okay
To do this again and again?
Behind a guise of justice, a fake name
That you wear to not look insane.

You people always think it's the 'us' that need to change
Society needs to accommodate you
You scream behind screens and never face anyone
Hiding from any real words that are true.

You think you have a right to ruin lives
To take away enjoyment 'cause you don't like it
To hunt and attack 'cause the masses turn a blind eye
To the behaviour that's truly toxic.

Has it never crossed your mind that you may be wrong?
Your views may be twisted and sickening?
But no, you're always in the right, aren't you?
'Cause of some other excuse to make you a victim.

It's wrong
It's all wrong
You are the problem in this society you try to change

You say again and again that it needs to change 'cause
there are problems that need to be addressed
Equality, acceptance, you wanna try affect them
Make it better for everyone but we all know
It's a lie.

Just because so many support you, you think it's right
But this ain't a battle you need to fight
The truth - if you let yourself see the light -
Is that you should change.

The world doesn't hold you down
You're the lucky ones born in nice cities and towns
While others truly suffer and drown
In hell zones that are dead all around.

Where the issues you preach of truly exist
Yet you keyboard warriors don't seem to notice.

You just want a world where only your kind exists
So you listen to only yourself and tear down anything that
opposes you.

So just think
For a second
Is that what we need for society?

Romeo Osei-Nyarko (13)
Robert Clack School Of Science, Dagenham

Corrupt Society And Honesty

When you go outside, what do you see?
The dull sky covering everyone's heart
While the joyful sun covers their faces
Too busy to even think of the weather
Can't even do a simple task.

When you go outside, what do you see?
Is it the young gossiping
While their future is in their hands, resting?
They all look amused,
But is that their true feeling?
No.
Explaining their feelings will blend in the wind,
Unheard of,
Then made into gossip, where they will regret,
Regret to express thoughts and feelings, it is not a bet,
But the truth.

When you go outside, what do you see?
Lies
Everyone is petrified to express themselves
But you shouldn't be
The truth is what everyone seeks
Not sharing honesty is a build-up of betrayal
But where is that confidence?
It's in your heart and mind
Imprisoned.

The key?
Your body, if it rejects or accepts.

Nowadays, your intentions
Are predicted through your acts and behaviour
How do you make people think incorrect of you?
You can't
Misjudged is not a term anymore
The only way is to act, corrupt or not
The way you look
Then that's where the word 'judged' is implied
It's everywhere, in everyone, but could be rid of
So how about you use the thoughts and feelings
That have been eating up your mind
To express who you are?

When you go outside, what do you see?
Misjudged
Everyone is a way different person than you think they are
A different past, a welcoming future.

Youhans Dilloo (14)
Robert Clack School Of Science, Dagenham

It's His Fault

Every step you take in the minefield is a chance to get hit,
Of course, it's me every time to get picked,
It's his fault,
But I'm the one getting kicked,
I'm the one getting thrown to the ground,
I'm the one who belongs in the lost and found,
I'm the one feeling like I'm about to drown,
I'm trying to swim up but he's pushing me back down,
It's his fault.
"Where's your dad?" they say. "Gone to get milk?"
Their laughter runs across my skin like silk,
They tell me he's been put five feet under,
The words vibrate through me like thunder,
They say that he thought I was a waste,
That I was misplaced and that I should have been replaced,
They ask me when he'll be back or will he ever?
I say no and probably never,
It's his fault,
They say I'm going to be alone forever.

No, no, I'm not alone,
I'm just waiting and waiting for my Dad to call me on his
phone,
Can't believe he's gone to a family in a different home,
It's just me and my mum, we can't do this on our own,
They say we need someone to support us,

Tell us who we are,
I sit and wonder where'd he go and how far?
Will he ever come back to tell me he loves me,
Or stay away and hide to never really see
The man I'll grow into, the man I wanna be?
I feel like I'm in prison and he's the key,
Why can't he come back and just set me free?
It's his fault,
But what if it's not,
What if it's my fault?

Harley Browning (13)
Robert Clack School Of Science, Dagenham

I Still Remember

I still remember all of the lies you sold me
I still remember all of the negativity you fed me
I still remember all of the people who you claimed would hold me
I still remember all the memories you turned cold for me
I still remember your sadistic grin as you remoulded me
I still remember the sting in your words
I still remember seeing myself on my deathbed
I still remember you distorting my head
I still remember thinking of pumping my body with lead
I still remember having to take those meds
I still remember trying to run from this inevitable dread
I still remember trying to run from my inevitable death
I still remember the hate you gave me
I still remember the dates that you left me
I still remember lying on my bed
I still remember how my thoughts were scattered
I still remember you kicking out the ones that truly mattered
I still remember how you made my happiness disappear
I still remember trying to get it to reappear, but I forgot you were my thoughts The Grim Reaper who was reaping my riches and planting sorrows
I still remember losing my friends
I still remember letting depression become my latest trend
I still remember feeling trapped in my own mind
I still remember losing myself in the night-time

I still remember it being my demons high-time
I still remember losing the battles
I still remember her helping me
And I also remember beating depression.

Alok Bhogal (14)
Robert Clack School Of Science, Dagenham

The True Monsters

You call me a madman,
You call me a creep,
You call me a lost cause,
You call me a freak.

You constrict me with your labels,
Your arsenal of names,
But I am truly your worst nightmare,
A person who does not fit into your frame.

Society's a jailer, not a spokesperson of the free,
I say, "P'shaw," when you guffaw at the monstrosity you say
is me,
However, with a sad tone, I must declare,
The true monsters are the name-callers
And they hunt everywhere.

There is a boy with a ruined face,
He was once proud and strong,
But fear and loneliness now stand in their place,
This was the work of the monsters we live among.

There was once a girl that her peers unkindly called 'J-J-J-
Joke',
Simply because the cowards made fun of her stutter when
she spoke.
Now she stands high, addressing the crowds aloud and
proud,

She is a beacon who says, "Once I was ridiculed, but look at me now!"

In the crowd stands out a hijab, so bright it could not be missed,
Sadly, the lady who wears it is passed by people hissing,
"Terrorist."
She is not a creature, nor an enemy of the state,
But a kind and honest citizen yearning to get respect, not hate.

Thus I end this poem on a hopeful thought,
Insults shall not harm us because out of confidence we are wrought!

Christopher Browne Maddox (13)
Robert Clack School Of Science, Dagenham

Be Careful When A Naked Person Tries To Give You A Shirt

You can never receive love from someone
When they don't retain it themselves
You will eventually realise you are just gaining emptiness.

Imagine pouring a lifetime into a relationship
Only to find out it was one-sided
Imagine pouring all the love you learnt from birth
Into a figure you thought of as a hero
Only to discover they would never dare blink an eye in your
direction
Now imagine this person - receiving all this compassion
Receiving all this care - has been labelling you as the enemy
'You' being the one who gave everything, what would be the
point in continuing?

What if the situation came to being embedded into living
with your supposed
'soulmate'
Whilst gripping onto your life with your last breath?
Would you still continue? Or is it too late?

You see, the problem I see is that multiple individuals
Have the disadvantage of not experiencing love in its true
form
It must have escalated to a point where they have nothing
to share

Absolutely nothing, so in return, they give us
Jealousy, anger, hate, negativity
You don't have anything to take away, they become useless.

But they still manage to tear down the thin wall
That keeps you apart from complete misery
Leaving you with absolutely nothing, you also become
useless.

Thinuja Thileepan (14)
Robert Clack School Of Science, Dagenham

Love Yourself

It's painful to look in the mirror
The *mask* that hides your pain looks so different
The weight of sealing your emotions weighs you down
Even though you can't cry, I know it hurts
The sky seems so diverse
Cold wind whispers a different story
Seasons keep on changing...
Yet, your cold heart stays melancholy.

Wings may be broken
And a *tear* may fall
As you *face yourself* and *wonder* about
Your mental health;
The most beautiful moment in life
May come when you
Wake up with an *epiphany*
And realise the *answer* is
You need to *love yourself*.

Don't pay attention to the world ending
It has ended for me many times
And began again the next morning.

You don't need someone else to validate your worth
Amidst the *sea* of countless voices
Please let your voice be heard
Learn to *love yourself* first before loving another human
being

Because when everything around you crumbles...
You only have yourself!

Loving yourself is not being selfish
It's embracing yourself for who you are...

Find yourself
Find your voice
Love yourself!

Tisha Rahman (14)
Robert Clack School Of Science, Dagenham

What Is Friendship?

A friend is someone you trust
Someone you rely on
Someone that is just
Like the ying in yang.

But is this all?
Is this all a friend is?
No.

A friend is family.

A sister
A brother
A mother
A father.

All can describe a friend
The moment you met each other
You knew they were there for you 'til the very end
As you will always be together.

They are the diamond to your jewellery
The earth to your sea
The branch to your berry
The leaves to your tree.

This is what a true friend is.

They will make you laugh a little louder

Your smile a little brighter
And your life a little better.

As true friends are impossible to forget
Because wherever you go
They will leave prints that will set
Into your heart that will always show.

Brighter than stars
Brighter than the moon.

As in the end
A friend is your chosen family
The keeper to your happiness
And a person with whom your bond is unbreakable.

This is the true meaning of friendship.

Jeehaan Dilloo (14)
Robert Clack School Of Science, Dagenham

Different Is Perfect

My dark skin was never a problem,
My ethnicity never an insecurity,
My identity never a part of my worries,
But they spoke and what was not an issue
Became something I was self-conscious of,
Almost ashamed of,
It was the comments,
How I was invisible in the darkness,
How being the darkest was somehow an insult,
It was the stare they gave me,
When I would show my roots,
It was the joke
That preyed on an insecurity I never knew I had,
It was every black male,
Obsessed with so-called 'lighties',
It was the curse of the standard of beauty,
I would look in the mirror and wonder why,
Why was it a problem to them?
Was it a problem to me?
Why did it matter the shade of brown my skin was?
How I looked?
Where I came from?
How did it affect anyone?
Why did we condemn each other?
Like we did when we sold each other as slaves.
People tan to get darker,

But my natural colour was a problem,
The melanin,
Eventually, we'll learn that
Everyone black is beautiful,
Everyone is different
And different is perfect.

Mary Ansong (14)
Robert Clack School Of Science, Dagenham

How Am I Not Good Enough?

How am I not good enough?
All these expectations need to turn into reality,
From him, her, they, I...
Being expected to look perfect all the time,
Makes me want to cry.
From all the make-up, clothes, hairstyles,
Where do I start?
How am I not good enough?
I see girls in school having the perfect body shape,
Acting like they didn't try at all,
How am I not good enough?
All the expectations need to turn into reality,
From him, her, they, I...
My feelings are gone,
Just like my confidence.
I try to look good for others,
Still sticking to the fashion trends,
How am I not good enough?
All these expectations need to turn into reality...
I hope...
I hope one day there will be no expectations,
I hope I don't need to take hours getting ready,
I hope that one day no one cares...
One day...
One day where being unique is beautiful,
One day where all skin colours are accepted,

One day where everyone is thought of as beautiful...
How am I not good enough?
All these expectations need to turn into reality.

Kalista Serdiukovaite (14)
Robert Clack School Of Science, Dagenham

It's Only Depression

It is only depression
She said
It's only a small mental illness
She said
Now they are gone...
However, you weren't the only one
Who said it was small.

When do people realise that
The things they say hurt?
When do people realise just because they are laughing and
smiling
Doesn't mean they are okay?

When you're surrounded by friends
But you feel alone
When you're meant to be happy
But you're empty inside.

I'm sorry I don't smile as much
Or laugh as much anymore
But when I do, it's to hide so much.

And now there are scars on my hips
And a smile on my lips
When most fear death
I pray for it.

I promised to tell you when I was sad
You asked me to
But I fear you getting bored
Of me saying it every day.

People don't understand
Depression, anxiety, suicide
Takes lives every day.

And now there are 'paper cuts'
All over my body
And people ask, "Do you have a cat?"

Neha Samplay (14)
Robert Clack School Of Science, Dagenham

That Bully In The Society

I can't believe it!
You have infected my brain and there is no cure
Why do you bully me?
You are destroying my life
Do you even know how I feel?
I feel like I am soaking in the sea
I feel so empty.

Stop!
This is driving me insane!
I can't handle this anymore!
You are destroying my life
Why?
You are making me feel trapped
Why don't you spend a day in my shoes?

You are fuelled with gloom and resentment
This is not like a movie where everything can be solved
This is real life
I feel downhearted, I feel unlucky, I feel miserable
You are destroying my life
You are so cheerful, carefree and contented about this.

Whoosh!
You are always looking for me to make me feel bad about
myself
You are destroying my life

I want to know how it feels to be free
Free from all of this!
I want to think that this is just a bad dream, but it's not.

Stop, listen and look
Your words don't hurt, they bleed!

Minahil Ubaid (14)
Robert Clack School Of Science, Dagenham

A Friend Called Depression

Please go away
Please leave me alone
I thought you were my friend
Getting through the struggles together
Right until the very end
You trapped me and changed me
I can't take this pain forever.

You stabbed me in the back
Left me sobbing on my own
There is one main thing you lack
To everyone, it is unknown.

You have left me neglected
Rejected from society
I hide you with a mask
Just like anxiety
I hope you know I suffer silently.

But my life is something that you intruded
For this, I have been left excluded
You've crushed me
You've snatched my freedom away
You've hurt me
I really wish you wouldn't stay.

The decisions you've made cannot be taken back
The past is the past

And that is that
So please be a true friend and hold me tight
As my future is not all that bright
It was not your fault, don't let anyone say different
The blame is to be given to a friend called depression...

Ellie-Kay Joan Taylor (14)

Robert Clack School Of Science, Dagenham

Social Media

Social media is the place people are fooled
Think that they need to look a certain way to look cool
Have idols who aren't who they seem to be
Try to be as good as their models and never roam freely
Why can't I look like that? I'm too fat
I will never look like that, I'm too flat.

But the real reason is that not everything is real
People who Photoshop others to break them down
Not caring about how it makes them feel
The victim keeps quiet in public but at home, all they do is
frown
The victim starts going crazy and losing their mind
But the suspect doesn't care and think it's worth their time
To make another person feel like they're drowning just to
have a laugh
The victim lies in bed trying not to barf
A joke that is said to be meaningless
Another person may take seriously.

So remember, don't believe everything you see online
And don't bully others on social media.

Akash Nath (13)
Robert Clack School Of Science, Dagenham

Friends

It's nice to have a good friend.

Friends are the family that we choose,
Friends make you laugh and are always there when you
need them the most,
They won't take your trust and betray it,
Friends should be by your side through it all, no matter
what.

True friends should defend and be loyal,
You see, loyalty is key,
It's a priceless gift that shouldn't be taken for granted,
And allow you to live to your best abilities and never put you
down.

Best friends should love you,
Even when you may be wrong, they will always have your
back,
Best friends should be the people you turn to
When you're upset, sad and lonely,
They should change that to make you happy,
To make you be the best that you can be.

Friends should make you laugh, let you live
And allow you to love,
If not, they aren't worth it.

Caitlin Davies (13)
Robert Clack School Of Science, Dagenham

I'm In Prison Without A Crime

I am in prison without fail
Every day of my life
People say that everyone must come here
But I strongly disagree.

Gangs and groups scattered around
Some merged into one
People say that everyone must serve the time
But I strongly disagree.

Four walls surround our areas
Even fences too
People say some get over
But I strongly disagree.

Fifty percent success rate
A number on these lives
People say they cannot lie
I strongly disagree.

Nothing compares to this torture
A useless set of skills
People say this is worth a lot
I strongly disagree.

It is said that no one can leave
Though some find a way
People say I should still care

I strongly disagree.

So next time you are near a prison
Think of the children inside
And what you felt
Then I might agree.

Sarah Haxell (14)
Robert Clack School Of Science, Dagenham

Coping

Coping, it's always the hard part, isn't it?
One day, that's all it takes for the world to turn upside down,
One breeze, then it came, now all you can do is cope,
Some people suffer from death and anxiety,
But I have to deal with every other kind of variety,
Now, now all we can ever do is cope.

Slowly, our bodies fade like shrivelled dust
And our depression soon enough becomes our obsession,
Where dreams become hopeless and our nightmares turn to reality
And now, now all we can ever do is cope.

However, there is more to us than our nightmares,
Our vivid dreams don't have to be our sob stories
And our schedules will never require therapies.
We can thrive, we can move like the wind's breeze
And now, and now, now all we can ever do is more,
More than ever just cope.

Muneeb Musharaf (14)
Robert Clack School Of Science, Dagenham

Racism

Racism has a human heart
An artery of cruelty and dark art
It has the blood of anger and wickedness
Has a force of pain and viciousness.

Some people carry their honour in a flag
And of their nationality, they brag
They feel superior and they differentiate
And against those who are different, they discriminate.

So many people still get judged by their race
For such, there never ought to be a place
Racism only leads to division and war
Just goes to show how ignorant some are.

At the end of the day
Our souls fly away
Are we all free now?
Are we all the same?

Though we live in a so-called democracy
Where's our freedom? Where's our privacy?
One day, the truth will shine
And everybody will realise the humanity that died.

Rand Ali Basha (14)
Robert Clack School Of Science, Dagenham

143

Poem

We live upon a blue globe,
With many problems to solve,
Problems we can't solve with the frontal lobe,
Proof that we will never evolve.

The corrupted earth of war,
With its share of death,
Death that will last for evermore,
Past our last breath.

The polar caps of the north,
Melting away into the oceans,
Filling up the Earth,
With a bunch of commotion.

Wars will spread,
Lives are lost,
Hearses for the dead
And lines are crossed.

Families separated,
Friendships end,
Governments incapacitated,
Loneliness the new trend.

We live upon an excuse for a home,
One with death as a way of life,

Where we are left in catacombs,
With people armed with knives...

Ahed Umair Gardaizi (14)
Robert Clack School Of Science, Dagenham

100 Days

I want to forget their names, the generals,
Advisors, puppet rulers,
The puffed-up and the brought-low.

I want not to know them,
Not hear their plans, their excuses,
The president and the president's men,
The Pope with this white smoke for voodoo.

The suits, ties, teeth, insignia,
The guns, the names of trucks and weapons.

I want to forget them all,
To be washed of them,
To begin again where no one knows who anyone is,
Or what he believes.

To give my attention to
Frangipani leaves curling,
The smell of jasmine,
One person helping another across a street.

To the seeds,
To the beginnings, to one clear word for which
There is no disguise and no alternative.

Charlie Cape (14)
Robert Clack School Of Science, Dagenham

What Have We Done?

This society we live in now
All these crimes we allow
When will we stop?
Is stopping an option for anyone here?
Or are you just going to talk about what happened there?
You don't care what's happening around
You stop, care and listen
For only then will this world glisten
All this corruption for what, just power?
What you're now doing is killing the Earth
You are the evil giving birth
To this darkness that we have to live in
This world will collapse because of you
You are responsible for your children's failure
You are the reason for all things death
You have ruined the future for the younger generation
This is what society has done, we have ruined our planet.

Imad Ahmed (14)
Robert Clack School Of Science, Dagenham

Division

Discrimination,
Division,
We are separated,
By actions,
That we had no control over.

Our skin,
Our accents,
Defined by someone,
Who we never knew,
Something,
We never experienced,
Yet still,
We're divided.

We are stuck,
Separated,
By borders,
We created,
We have no control,
Of how we live,
Currently.

They chose,
How we live,
Why we stay,
Entitled

And isolated,
Rather than together
And united.

Discrimination,
Division,
They are words of the past,
Yet still,
With relevance,
More than most words.

We must change this,
For them.

Logan Allen (14)
Robert Clack School Of Science, Dagenham

Mom And Dad

You are the ball of joy that lights me up
You are the one I lean upon
You are the one who taught me life
How not to fight and the difference between right and
wrong
You are the words within my song
You are my wonderful dad.

You are the ones who care for me
You are the eyes that help me see
I'm afraid of life but looking for love
I'm blessed that God sent me you from above
You are my friend, my heart, my soul
You are the greatest mom I know.

You two are both from Heaven and
I have been blessed to have you both.

Love from me is forever circling you
And forever it will be, Mom and Dad.

Rida Syeda Noor (13)
Robert Clack School Of Science, Dagenham

Bullying

We need to stop it,
It's not good,
Harassment,
Can lead to many things,
Suicide,
Death is not the answer,
But many do.

Stop bullying,
It does not help,
Not yourself,
Don't make you happy,
Is it something you should
Be proud of?

It's a shame people are bullied,
Because of how they look,
Dress,
Or act,
It's a shame they bully you,
But it's all okay because
We just hide,
Letting them keep pushing and pushing.

To the point,
To the point where death
Is the answer for some.

Lacey Summer Tier (14)
Robert Clack School Of Science, Dagenham

151

Someone Tell Me

We are all human, all the same
We all have, two arms, two legs and two eyes
But why do we treat each other differently?
Someone tell me,
Is it because I am black, white, Asian,
Mexican, African, Chinese, Japanese?
Someone tell me
Why do we treat each other differently?
Someone, please tell me
Is it how I look, how I speak?
Where I am from, the colour of my skin?
Someone tell me
Someone tell me why
I'll tell you this, one day, someone told me
He told me that we'll never know.

Endri Halili (14)
Robert Clack School Of Science, Dagenham

The Cries Of A Thousand Men

Boom!
Boom is the sound of doom.
Men yelp in fear,
They run out of their trenches,
Only to smell foul stenches.
This disgusting aroma was made by the dead;
These men wish they could go home and sleep in their
comfortable beds.
But this is war...
They're fighting for more,
Boom!
The sound of doom.
The trenches summon the men to return;
They do -
Just like a fox returns to its den.
All you can hear is
The cries of a thousand men.

Umar Khilji (14)
Robert Clack School Of Science, Dagenham

For Honour

Honour, what do you know about honour?
When life becomes motionless in the heart of battle,
Screams of your comrades, enemies,
While walking down the thin, red path,
When your heart stops with the beginning of sorrow
And countless lives are lost to conflict.

Traumatised,
Forced to clutch your sword and shield,
To charge into the unknown,
But your enemies will remember your name and
Will quiver in fear, to fight for your country
And to die with honour.

Thomas Webb (14)
Robert Clack School Of Science, Dagenham

Racism

Racism.
When will it end?
Can't we join forces
And be each other's friend?
No, we can't because of labels
Labels that need to be forgotten about,
Never used again!
But will that ever happen?
No, because babies, young like cubs
Grow up in a world full of labels.

Racism.
A terrible thing.
It will forever be outraging,
Don't you dare be beat down by it,
You are you,
Not what others say you are,
Never forget that.

Dipo Eweoya (13)
Robert Clack School Of Science, Dagenham

Friendship To Me

The ones who are dear to my heart
It will be a tragedy for us to be apart
I can never be away from these people
I see them as my equals.

The ones I trust the most
I know they hold me close
To some, friendship comes easy
To me, it's harder to please me.

A good friendship starts with trust in each other
There's always things to discover about one another
A friend will always watch your back
And carry the load so it doesn't crack.

Jessica Cook (13)
Robert Clack School Of Science, Dagenham

The Bending Of The Mind

The difficult state of mentality
Can honestly bend our reality
And can make us see things morbid
When you let your mind run into orbit.

It can make you see what isn't there
No matter how deeply you glare
And it can ruin your night's sleep
No matter how high or how deep.

These things truly are the state of mind
And stick with even the highest of mankind
And they come in a rage of variety
Like depression, suicide and even anxiety.

Joseph Palmer (14)
Robert Clack School Of Science, Dagenham

157

Friend

I wanted to thank you
But was unable to explain
What it means to me
To have a friend
To share life's joys and life's pains
I'll be there when you are crying
You will be there when I'm smiling
Thank you for standing by my side
When no one else would
You never seem to judge me
You never put me down
You put a smile on my face
When you see a frown
Thank you.

Chloe Brooks (14)
Robert Clack School Of Science, Dagenham

Would You Look At Me?

Would you look at me the same
If I was white?
Would you look at me the same
If I was black?
Would you even look at me?

But you don't know their background
And everything they have been through
Don't look at them differently because of
How they dress and
How they look.

No one knows their stories and tales
You don't know...
No one does.

Freddy Joe Ling (13)
Robert Clack School Of Science, Dagenham

The Young Girl

Once was a rainy day
There, the young girl lay
She struggled a lot
She had a lot of money, not!

She didn't have a family
Nor did she have a home
She would sit in the rain
And get hit by all sorts of stones.

So here we are, talking about the girl
Talking about how she struggled
One day, struggling won't be a thing
Hustling will.

Kyle Irving (14)
Robert Clack School Of Science, Dagenham

A Drought Of Happiness

Happiness doesn't last, it stops and resets from the start
Like a CD which skips all the best parts
But I was fine in the past until it hit me at the age of ten
Left me wondering if I'll ever love myself again
I ain't happy to be me, I'd rather see the world through
someone else's eyes
Than have those same eyes look at me
I cry to realise the pain of why I've woken up again
I'd rather be six feet under than waking up at six in the
morning
Getting ready to hear all these lies about how life is so great
I'm too scared to take my own life away
But the question I still ask myself, knowing that the demons
rage
When they hear me say, "Why can't I just be happy?"

Ashleen Mpambawahle (13)

St Edward's CE School & Sixth Form College, Romford

161

The Perfect Society

Welcome to society,
Where your dreams are shattered before they're made
And our freedom doesn't match our realities,
Where we judge each other and begin to hate
And our standards are higher than we could ever reach,
Never telling us to see our true potential.

Welcome to society,
Where our self-esteem is broken by someone's sins,
Where we fail to see life, only colour,
So we begin to despise the people we were born as.

Welcome to society,
Where we are forced to be who we are not,
Where stereotypes become the truth
And our problems are never acknowledged,
Until it's too late.

Welcome to society,
Where our lives are decided by status
And money is the only thing we live for,
So we succeed or die pursuing it.

Welcome to society,
Where we live in a system designed to kill us,
Where we don't look forward to the future,
As we destroy the Earth we call home.

Wait!
Why are you leaving already?
We welcome you with open arms
Until you don't live up to our expectations,
So we taunt you 'til you decide to die
And bury you with a web of lies.

Scary, right?

Ogechi G Ugoji (13)
St Edward's CE School & Sixth Form College, Romford

My Hero

My hero doesn't have powers
My hero doesn't judge
My hero doesn't have a sidekick
My hero doesn't care about colour
My hero doesn't ask for help to just show off
My hero will keep us children safe
My hero will care for everyone
My hero isn't a hero, my hero is a heroine.

Keziah Edward (12)
St Edward's CE School & Sixth Form College, Romford

We Are Here

We are here, sitting in a school,
We are here, in a crisis because the Wi-Fi won't work,
But there are people out there with no education,
People out there with no work,
People out there who can't feed their children,
People out there who can't feed.

We are here, taking food for granted,
We are here, taking love for granted,
But there are people living in poverty,
Nothing to do but lie on the streets quietly
And wait until it's time to go
And live with their fallen family.

We are here, friends to laugh with,
We are here, money to bask in,
But there are people who are homeless,
People out there with no money
And what do we do?
We do nothing to help them.

I believe that this can be stopped,
Stop poverty and save them from rot,
We are here, living a normal life,
Not caring about those on the street,
But we can change, treat everyone equal
And finally end poverty... forever.

Jesse Ayres (11)
St John The Baptist School, Kingfield

Wondrous Witch

Dirty, green skin
Tall, towering and thin,
A heart of stone,
The reason she's alone,
Black, pointy hat,
Making potions out of a rat,
Wickedly evil is the witch,
Bonding magic,
Causing tragic,
Wherever she goes,
She makes everyone twitch.

Stirring mysterious mixtures,
Spitting, bubbling and staring at creepy pictures,
The old woman may not be
As horrible and terrifying as we all see.

Remarkably, she helps the sick,
Quickly then leaps up onto her broomstick,
Her disgusting yet magnificent mixtures heal,
But whatever she does,
As hard as she tries,
She barely has enough for a meal.

Inside the small, old village,
Generously, the lady does all she can,
Brewing medicines, helping everywhere, cleaning all and any
spillage,

But none, not one fan
Does she have.

Patchy roof, battered and broke,
Small cottage of oak,
Rotting floorboards
And never any rewards.

Kind-hearted, polite, gentle, caring,
Warm-hearted, considerate, helpful, understanding,
Tender, patient, giving, sympathetic, loving,
What a marvellous and inspiring lady she is,
But not a lot see this,
She does all she can to help in the village,
But she gets nothing in return, an unpleasant image.

Kindly, the miraculous woman gives everything she has,
But to receive in return, she is the last.

Terrifying sight, she may be a bit,
Black cloak, black cat,
Black shoes, black hat,
Green skin,
Body lean and thin,
Big toes,
Crooked nose,
Warts on her face,
But none of this matters,
She has the best heart of all for starters,

Her heart is like a glowing moon,
Courteous, understanding, gracious,
Humble, gentle, wondrous and generous,
A witch she may be,
But the best of them all,
Incredibly, she is a star, shining bright in the night,
You will finally see,
Definitely, the old lady is surely not cruel.

Oliwia Ziemak (11)
St John The Baptist School, Kingfield

The Old Man

I saw the old man almost every day
He was heartless, he was mean
But I could see
That inside he was beautiful, perhaps like a tree
He was strange, that old man whom I saw every day
Slept with his horses, so they say.

I saw sadness in his eyes
Whenever he'd come by
They'd been through a lot, suffered from lies
Sometimes I'd hear him in the middle of the night
I woke because of his sad cries.

He always had a space in his heart for me
I was the child he never had, but I will never be
He had no friends, he had no money nor family
He never spoke of his wife
I knew he loved her his whole life.

I knew he voyaged when he was young
And I knew he had failure in his right lung
His life went downhill after that
He got pushed, he got shoved
He lived life well although never loved.

I miss the old man and I hope he has healed
His name was Ben
And I never saw him again.

Elani Isabella Bidessie-Mistretta (12)
St John The Baptist School, Kingfield

Depression No More

He stopped breathing
Help, help, help!
His family ran straight to him and took him to the hospital
What did he do? It turned out it was cancer
No one could predict it was going to happen
His lungs had filled with fluid in his sleep.

In his sleep, he would have nightmares from this illness
His mother would cry her eyes out every night
She had to get sleeping pills
His sister would actually care for him, pray for him
But his father, he didn't care at all, all he would do is swear,
glare, not care.

There came the chance when he had to go back to school
Everyone would care
All they did was care, care, care.

Then one day, when big bullies got in his way
They told him, "Hey you, watch your way!"
Every time he passed their corridor, he would run, run, run.

The bullies saw him run, run, run
They kept thinking, *this is so much fun*, but why?
Because he was the weak one.

This made him depressed
He wanted to be the best

But instead, he was just a mess
They just needed to give it a rest.

The boy had an idea to end his depression
He could just go
And never return
So all this could end.

He almost did it
Then someone stopped it
A young pretty girl, she was a therapist and the merriest
Did he want to be like her?
Yes, because she was the best!
No one thought odd of her.

He went with the therapist
Told her his story
She was a benefit.

By the end of the year
He was a mess no more.

Poppy Phin (11)
St John The Baptist School, Kingfield

Silence

Silence
It is evil
Always there, daring you to take a knife and cut right
through it
It may always be there, shouting in your face
Telling you that no one will like your idea or what you want
to say
Or the silence might be saying not to share your feelings
But to put them in a bottle and hide it where no one can
find it
Letting your feelings rot away in your pain
Sadness or longing all alone,
Waiting for you to find the knife.

Your head may already be waiting for you
To voice your thoughts to let them run free in the world
But you may be doubtful, scared that
The translucent tendrils of doubt may wrap its suckers
Around your throat, suffocating your voice
And burying your thoughts or feeling deep down in your
head
Never letting it out, bad thoughts clouding your head.

I look back at the times when these thoughts were mine and
laugh
I am now one with the silence, it is my friend
The silence gives me time to think

Clear my thoughts so I am ready to voice them
Once you find your voice, sing your feelings from the
rooftops
Confident and proud that silence cannot harm you.

They may be little or they may be big
That doesn't matter, every thought counts
Never let the silence stop you from doing what you want
Don't let those wispy tendrils block your voice
Or drown your thoughts with bad ones
Instead, just speak, let your thoughts roam the world
To find someone to inspire
Never let silence control you.

Ella Browne-Kaempf (11)
St John The Baptist School, Kingfield

Fragile Families

When you come back from school, feeling all down
Your parents are at home and they certainly won't frown
You can hold them with your hands and lean on their shoulder
Always there for you, even when you're older
Their warmth will surround you throughout the day
Never-ending love, come what may.

If your loved ones weren't there
Would you really care?
As you wouldn't have anyone
It would rain and not be fun.

Every day when you wake up, you know there'll be a meal
But no one really understands, it's quite a big deal
Your parents work hard for you, even in rough times
Going to buy food for you - including limes
When you look at your plate and see what you're eating
You are kept nice and warm with lots of heating
Smile at your parents, let them know you actually care
Watch their loving expression and really start to stare
They're the ones who will always be with you - thick and thin
Always look after what you get and try not to throw food in the bin.

As tears drip down your face
You slow down the pace

Everything comes to a stop
Then you start to drop
But you see your sister
Who gave you a blister
Do you understand?
It was all planned
Your family will be with you
Through all the times you're blue
Families are fragile, hold them in your heart!

Kathleen D'Costa (12)
St John The Baptist School, Kingfield

High School Drama

During human years,
We come to the fear
Of the disastrous high school drama,
Children come to an age
Of a maturing stage
And learn to deal with the trauma.

If it's making words go to your head,
Or abhorrent rumours bound to spread,
Soon, it will come to cut the thread,
Echoing, embedding every word that they said,
Or if it's to break serenity -
A bond lasting centuries,
The penalty for jealousy
Is turning friends to enemies.

The high school drama will seal a fate,
With corrupted minds, she will contaminate,
The undercover architect or to disconnect,
Disrespect and to reject,
When you wonder how this will affect
The reason that you're not perfect
And that's why you deflect,
Kind actions of respect.

She will break the balance between love and hate
And cause a problematic debate

On why your homework's due late
Because you couldn't say you procrastinate.

This mould will soon be drying,
Drugs, people keep buying,
Fights that end up with crying,
Teachers students keep defying,
Backstabbing and lying,
Pupils' spirits will soon be dying,
Forget the high school drama,
With its grief and strife,
Because soon, you'll be older,
Looking back on that life.

Yzabella Laguisma (11)
St John The Baptist School, Kingfield

Animals

We are animals
Animals are us
We destroy
We rebuild
We kill.

We waste animals
We chuck them away
We treat them like trash
We don't care
We kill.

Thinking we're in danger
Well, no
We are the danger
We don't let them live
We kill.

We should let them be free
Let them live their lives
For we all have only one
Even cats
Let them live.

Help us understand
That we are animals
And animals are us
Let's follow the animal kingdom's rules

Don't kill.

The nets that animals fear
Trapped inside them
Waiting for their death
Let's stop
Don't kill.

Arrows of death
Soaring through the air
Hitting the golden heart
Of the innocent
Don't kill.

Death curls around us like a scarf
Pulling animals near
Making them die out
We are the monsters
Don't kill.

Mythical creatures hide
Putting their glory away
So that we won't hurt
So that we won't kill
Don't kill.

We think animals are monsters
Because they slash their claws
But they aren't monsters
They just protect themselves

And their families
Please don't kill.

Sophia Bocer (12)
St John The Baptist School, Kingfield

Poaching

As the last honey-glazed rays of light
Sprawl across the sky
The landscape is dyed rose gold
The moon settles in like a cat on a windowsill
A glow of chrome silver floods in
The scenery now an ocean of polished mirrors
The silence is deafening
No signs of movement through the darkness
Everything lifeless.

In the distance, appears a baby sun
It is imprisoned
Much like the animals here in the Kalahari
Not one poor beast will see the light of day again
They went into the cage
That would be their last breath in the real world
Once you were aimed with a silver stick
You would be surrounded by millions more.

Focus through binoculars instead of guns
Spectate their beauty but not only to design
A priceless skin purse
There is space for more than just human species
There is still a gap to be filled
It's empty and it's waiting for a new beginning.

Teresa Sanchez (12)
St John The Baptist School, Kingfield

The Old World

Change your opinion on things,
What looks like a devil could have wings.
Don't judge a book by its cover,
Don't judge a friend by their lover.
Things aren't always what they seem,
Take time to really know them.

The sun does not help us,
It causes a fuss,
So why do we respect the sun and resent rain?
It doesn't mean we love fun but hate tears,
The world was not made to be judged,
So why has our opinion been smudged?

Everything has changed,
Everyone just wants to exchange,
We crave money
And no longer find family important,
Why does the world have to be like this?
It is the old world I miss.

Anti-social they call it - technology,
We should spend time doing geology,
I ask you all to be kind
And everything starts with your mind,
So think!
Does it matter if their parents are that?

Stop accusing each other,
Be kind and act like a mother,
"It wasn't her!"
"It was him!"
Everyone give tolerant advice,
Hopefully, that will break the ice.

Because back in the old world,
The water swirled,
People moved freely,
I could be me.
So why does the world have to be like this?
It is the old world I miss.

Catherine Henn (11)
St John The Baptist School, Kingfield

The Girl On The Swing

I remember when I joined school
I remember the crown of thorns
My 'friends' put on my eyes
So I could never see them take off their masks
The times they sewed my mouth so the letters
B-U-L-L-I-E-S or H-E-L-P
Never escaped
The wax they melted to block my ears shut
I never really did hear anything
Only a muted mumble...
I let them hold my rose once
I kept it in a fragile glass
When I gave it to them, they shattered it
Peeling the petals off one by one
Piece by piece
That moment scarred me quite literally
It made me play with knives and scissors near my skin
Like a puppeteer
Sticks and stones near my bones
I was crying for help in the asylum in my mind
But tears drowned me and chains and anvils
Marked 'life' dragged me down, so I gave up
On seeing a glimpse of light
She said she was fine but isn't it all one
Puzzle in the teenage mind?
It's society that killed her

Not even being noticed because of the screens
And the movies and beauty
Not even by her parents, engulfed in politics and staring
She sat on a swing with broken wings
Writing her story with pain.

Sofia Lorraine Sarao (12)
St John The Baptist School, Kingfield

Snakes

If you are not aware of snakes,
Then now's the time to learn,
Some snakes are harmless,
Well, to humans,
Others, not so much.

The black mamba is deadly,
Deadly enough to subdue even the strongest man,
The inky black inside its mouth
Might be the last thing you see.

All that you need to know is that,
Not all snakes are dangerous,
Whereas others could kill you,
A snake will flee if given the chance to,
But if cornered, watch out,
For it will bite.

The Mozambique spitting cobra
Is the champion archer,
When threatened, it will shoot,
Or worse, it will bite.

So if you see a snake,
Do not kill it with a rake.

As the longest snake in Africa,
The forest cobra is a formidable threat,

Also a member of the feared four,
His hood a danger sign,
Get back or I'll bite.

So if you see a snake, think of it from the snake's point of
view,
Respect this creature,
Treat it with respect and give it space and time
And before you worry about being bitten,
Don't forget you live in Britain.

William Ezzard (12)
St John The Baptist School, Kingfield

The Challenger

A great escape from the outside world
A regular-sized cube with nine tiles on each side
The more you move the tiles
The more you think, the harder it gets.

A great agitation to all the stress
A mental escape from all the weight
All the worries that fill your head are gone
You think all the complications are gone.

This great puzzle that was on top
Brings joy to all the children but this cube
Is so unique to my life
It is a diversion to anxieties.

A wave of rage
And a blow of relief
And a gust of entertainment
And a punch of challenge.

The cube waits and waits
It is a pet waiting for you to feed it
You turn and turn the sides of the cube
The tiles get confused.

You try and try to sort the tiles with the correct colours
But everything goes wrong
It is as stressful as fighting a tiger

You quit but you soon pick it back up.

The cube glares at you
Begging you to solve it
Except that you think it's impossible
It's a Rubik's cube.

Kristian Guardiana (12)
St John The Baptist School, Kingfield

Scars

I feel like I'm being shot every single day
By the names you call me
You laugh
I cry
I can't show that on the outside
But I show my scars.

Say I'm faking it, say I just want attention
Am I really?
How would you know?
Do you see my gunshot wounds?
Do you see my scars?
No, you don't.

'Sticks and stones will break my bones, but words will not'
Don't say to me that words will not break me
Because sometimes, they do
My friend's verbal plaster work, temporarily
They eventually fall off to let me bleed and die inside.

The pills you prescribe won't help me or my sanity
They form me
But it's not really me
It's your ideal version of me
I'm probably 99% anti-depressants and 1% me.

But I've risen up
Like the sun in the sky or moon rising in the night

I never fitted into a mould
So I moulded my own
But my scars will always show through.

Keira Borlagdatan (11)

St John The Baptist School, Kingfield

Riverdale

Riverdale, the town with pep
Take another step
From the outside, it looks like an innocent town
From the inside, you do nothing but frown.

Our story begins early on the 4th of July
The sun blazing hot
But a good day this was not
The Blossom twins sailed down sweet water river
The ice-cold water made them shiver.

But as the rain fell and the thunder roared
This day was not good anymore
Like a dazzling dream
To a dangerous nightmare
Like a calm river
To a ferocious sea.

As blood was poured and screams were deafening
The amount of tears that were cried that day
Could fill an ocean.

Two hours later, on the shore
A girl with hair as bright as the sun
Sat on a rock as grey as the clouds
On the outside, she might have seemed tough
But no one knew the horrors she'd seen.

Her world got turned upside down
On that fatal morning on the 4th of July
They are not the Blossom twins anymore.

Freya Willis (11)
St John The Baptist School, Kingfield

Grateful

Walking through the battlegrounds,
Fighting for what is right,
The country is theirs for the taking,
No matter how much their body is aching,
Through wind, rain and snow,
The sounds they hear are the worst type of blows,
A cross on their back,
No difference between white and black,
With every sound,
Comes a risk,
Just one,
Working all day for us,
Protecting not themselves, but all,
They will never feel small,
Will they ever get home?
But we know,
That they know,
We are grateful for their sacrifice,
And how their lives shaped ours,
If they return,
Hearts start to churn,
Bear hugs and kisses,
Chocolates and sweets of all shapes and sizes,
Lying in bed,
Led by all thoughts and feelings,
Nightmares of death, friends and death,

Tossing and turning,
Fear in their stomach burning,
But we know,
That they know,
We are grateful for their sacrifice
And how their lives shaped ours.

Rosina Waplington (12)
St John The Baptist School, Kingfield

What Was There?

I looked through my window one morning
To see what was there that day
There were bushes and trees
Mountains of leaves
And dinosaurs wandered the plains.

I looked through my window one morning
To see what was there that day
There were craters all over
A giant space ogre
And the ground was rocky and grey.

I looked through my window one morning
To see what was there that day
And fish swam past
A shipwreck's old mast
And sleeping mermaids quietly lay.

I looked through my window one morning
To see what was there that day
I saw myself standing tall
Covered in medals and all
And everyone was cheering, "Hooray!"

I looked through my window one morning
To see what was there that day
My garden stood still
I put my elbows on the windowsill

And imagined what was there that day.

Look through your window one morning
To see what you'll see that day.

Akane Hincapie (12)
St John The Baptist School, Kingfield

Rugby Is Great

I am carried, kicked and thrown,
I am dived on and I need answers,
What did I ever do to you?
I don't groan in pain,
I don't run away,
And this is how you repay me!

All the men around me jump, scramble and shout,
Yet, they don't dare pout,
The headbands on the players ask,
Why do you play this game?
Is it for the fame?
And I reply, "No, it's because rugby is my game."

I am a cone-shaped egg,
Fragile, yes, but I can't be compressed,
I don't care who you are
Or where you're from,
But with some luck and if you show some skill,
I will respond.

The precious skill you need is
Belief,
You don't need to be the biggest or the quickest,
Just a heart the size of a street,
I teach you the best thing,
Even those who are beaten are not defeated,

"What goes on tour no longer stays on tour,
It stays with you for life."

Blair MacKenzie (11)
St John The Baptist School, Kingfield

She Can't Find The Words

If she could speak
Everyone hears but no one will listen
The secrets fill her up and haunt her
Until she can't take it anymore.

She goes to events but no one knows she's there
Where she is forced to vote for someone
Who has been labelled popular
Someone who has caused her so much pain.

They know it's wrong
They know she feels like she doesn't belong
Yet, they stand there
Looking, whispering, calling.

She lies there in her tears
Wishing that she could disappear
She builds up walls
That even she can't break
Because remembering is the worst kind of pain.

When the last speck of hope, happiness is gone
When she tries to hold on
When she is at the end of the road
When there is nowhere to go.

The tragic, unthinkable story spreads
People mourning, full of regret

They hunt their next victim
Until it happens again.

Kate Eleanor Hinton (12)
St John The Baptist School, Kingfield

Why Am I Not Good Enough?

Mahatma Gandhi once said
"You yourself as much as anybody in the entire universe
Deserves your love and affection."

So why am I not good enough?
Is it because of my race?
Is it because of how I look?
Is it my clothes?
Is it because of my gender?
Or is it because I don't hate the latest trend?

I wake up every day thinking, *why was I born this way?*
These long dresses
These short skirts
These heavy shirts
To me, it is just wrong.

Your mind is useful
How many doors do I have to unlock
'Til I actually appreciate myself?
How many times do I have to be in this mental prison
Overthinking a solution to change my body?

Because the only doors that exist
Are in your mind
And all you have to do is work through them.

So I have one question for you
Why do you not appreciate yourself?

Rai Hilary Mandizha (12)
St John The Baptist School, Kingfield

The Bully

The bully was strong and fierce
I was... I was the fat one, the ugly one
Scared and weak, I never spoke or peeked.

My teacher would notice the notes in my tray
The hurts and the pain, I know it's a shame
It doesn't really rhyme, but it's okay.

Mum would ask me, "How was your day?"
I would just shrug my shoulders and run away
I lied to my parents so I could hide.

I told the bus driver to scoot away
Far from home
Never to see the mean ones again.

Three years later, I am on the streets living in pain
People stop to stare
Some share but really they don't care.

Stealing money and bread, living dangerously
Should I be living this way at fourteen?
Or should it be time?

I start to look at myself, I want to die
I lied to my family so I could hide
What am I thinking...?

Isabel Caamano (12)
St John The Baptist School, Kingfield

Nature

Do you know why animals become extinct?
Do you know why different, unique animals die each year?
I'll tell you why...
Over 3.5 billion to 7 billion trees are cut down each year
Which means 'you' are destroying animals' habitats
Such as bats and birds
What if 'you' were in their shoes?
What if 'you' were that animal?
Imagine you were a bird
Flying in the air peacefully, looking for food
Then you come back in the hot afternoon as the sun blazes
'You' couldn't find your nest
Where could it be?
Did you miss it?
Then you see trees come crashing down to the ground
As people cut them down with their razor-sharp chainsaws
How would you feel as a bird?
It's not only birds, it's other animals too
'Cutting down trees will leave future generations breathless'.

Kevin New (11)
St John The Baptist School, Kingfield

The Sea Is Full Of Surprises

The sea is full of surprises,
You never know what's next,
The weary waves roll in and out,
It's an instrument of death.

The sea is full of surprises,
An angel that makes you laugh,
Its ancient mind will not forget,
You'll be safe, away from harm.

The sea is full of surprises,
A monster that won't go away,
It sings and sings to lure you there,
You won't see the light of day.

The sea is full of surprises,
A friend that's always there,
If trouble ever finds a way,
You'll always be a pair.

The sea is full of surprises,
It sends shivers down your spine,
If someone drowns in the murky depths,
You know it is a sign.

The sea has many qualities,
Many colours like azure and jade,

Though remember what is written here,
Beware or you will pay.

Aviano Bastin (11)
St John The Baptist School, Kingfield

Butterfly

Wriggling and jiggling,
I'm a lonely log of green,
I haven't any family,
I don't wish to be seen.

Squirming up a cabbage,
I munch on one leaf,
I hear a voice yelling,
"That annoying, little thief!"

I find a nice, little ledge
And hang upside down,
I feel dizzy at first,
But now I can see the entire town.

I encase myself in silk,
Taking my last breath,
I plunge into the darkness,
Will it lead to death?

After a long while,
I feel strange and odd,
I break out of my cage,
Is this an act of God?

I have a whole new body,
I feel stiff and tired,
Antennae and four legs,

But my wings are what I admired.

All different colours,
Green, yellow, red and blue,
I'm more pretty,
Than the animals at the zoo.

Jessie Nicholl (12)
St John The Baptist School, Kingfield

Top 15 In 100 Dogs 2019

So in the top fifteen comes Cavachon, when it comes to
them, no need for caution
Number fourteen, Dandie Dinmont, legs not bandy
Number thirteen, Labradoodle, not quite a poodle
Number twelve, miniature schnauzer, barks a little bit louder
Number eleven, flat-coated retriever, retrieves the cleaner
Number ten, mixed breed, do a range of mixed deeds
Number nine, golden retriever, a tail like a beaver
Number eight, German shepherd, slower than a leopard
Number seven, Border collie, hair like a dolly
Number six, boxer, acts like a boxer
Number five, cocker spaniel, top of the annual
Number four, springer spaniel, bring something personal
Number three, Labrador, dog or friend
Number two, cockapoo, the chosen few
Number one, Staffordshire bull terrier, their smiles are
merrier
For all those dog lovers, they are the top dogs!

Melissa Eden Daisy Dommett (11)
St John The Baptist School, Kingfield

I Don't Get It

When you label me
'Different', 'weird' or 'fat'
I don't get it
When many are racist and find it abnormal
For people to be darker than them
But when the grocery store
Sunbed store or your local beach
Can make you look like me.

Why is it
We are building walls but not bonds?
When people look different they are labelled terrorists
When is that a label?
When living on the streets is a symbol of nothing
Nobody dares to spare a coin.
When we don't provide the resources for education
For those who need it most.
When we only allow one gender to get all the credit.
When we let people just be quiet about their worries and
their anxiety gets the best of them.
When we don't listen to the young people of today
I don't get it.

Augustine Kaitharath (12)
St John The Baptist School, Kingfield

Cancer Memories

As I sit on the hospital bed
The machine behind me
Goes *bleep, bleep, bleep!*
I look around
To see my mum
With a warming smile
Cancer may take claim to my
Outer shell
But never
Comes close to my fragile soul
Cancer cannot destroy hope
It cannot shatter dreams
It cannot steal spirit
It cannot conquer eternal life
My soul will jump, run, leap
Over attempts of cancer to pull me down
Those who surround me
Will fight with me
You see, cancer
You do not own me
You see illness
I see hope
It cannot cease memories
Cancer makes me think
Of all the good times
I've had

And won't take over
I own my body
Myself
And I will survive
Love is all around me
Love can survive death
While cancer can't.

Elyse Ryder (12)
St John The Baptist School, Kingfield

Football Is A Sport For Me

Football is a sport for everyone to play,
So why doesn't everyone have their say?
It's only a game,
Who cares about fame?
Football is a sport for me!

Scoring a goal is great,
But have you thought about your mate?
He sets you up with a beautiful pass,
Skimming across the newly-cut grass,
Football is a sport for you!

Past one defender, maybe one more?
Should I pass to my teammate or just ignore?
Just remember this is a team sport,
The best you could say, apart from the baggy shorts!
Football is a sport for everyone!

Football is my favourite sport by far,
But it really is depressing when the ball flies over the bar,
Football stars have a talent
And on TV, it's really apparent
Football is a sport for me!

Michael Okon (11)
St John The Baptist School, Kingfield

Beasts Far Below

Drowned in wonder, yet hidden by mist,
Murky and dark and still sunkissed,
Clear through the eyes, a blur in the mind,
To perplex one's thoughts, this world was designed.

Like a serene summer, it is born from a shower,
Like vibrant joy, it can change within the hour,
Like the tender tide that glistens with grace,
Abruptly, our Earth could prove it's two-faced.

A lack of us can comprehend,
Our bliss and our terror are far from their end,
An absence of fear could see us through,
Still, our suffering continues where doves once flew.

A plot of destruction by beasts far below
Has now become apparent, universally known.
Occasionally, they announce their presence
And we are stolen, unarmed and hesitant.

Sarah Wates (12)
St John The Baptist School, Kingfield

Friendship

Friendship is like a puzzle,
You need to find the perfect match,
Some go on forever but some will crash,
Don't judge people from the outside,
Take a look inside,
See what they are really like,
You may be surprised.

Hard times aren't so bad,
When you have a friend by your side,
You will go through some rough moments,
When you may feel it has ended.

But once it is,
This bond you have been creating,
Don't forget those memories,
The fun you have been making,
You may be sad,
But it is not so bad,
Think of the future,
More friends to meet.

People can be selfish, others may be kind,
But don't forget to look deep inside,
To find out who they really are!

Emma Lobb (12)
St John The Baptist School, Kingfield

The Streets We Used To Run

Back then you could roam the street
Now we wander in fear
With no one we think is safe near
Gazing and staring
Looking for someone who is caring.

How do you know that alleyway is safe?
How can you trust the person over there?
They could leave you feeling bare
Taking everything you own
How do you know that you will be left alone?

As the darkness settles on the paths and walls
The lower their patience falls
They are ready to stab and steal
Create wounds that cannot heal
Hiding in the shadows, conceal
They don't care how you feel.

We ask why
Why make us cry?
For what they take
Is no mistake
This is what has come
Of the streets we used to run.

Imogen Ryan (11)
St John The Baptist School, Kingfield

Is It Us To Be Afraid?

You say you're afraid of sharks and spiders
But is it us to be afraid?
You say you're afraid of tigers and rhinos
But is it us to be afraid?
Maybe
Just maybe
They're afraid of us
They're hunted
They're wanted
We cut down the trees
We pollute the seas
We destroy their homes
The fish
The chimpanzees
All the beauty
Could all be gone
Beasts
Monsters
The names you call them
Have you ever thought that
Maybe
Just maybe
We're the real monsters?
Maybe
They're like us
They may not speak our language

Or walk like us
But
They have feelings too
So I say save the animals
Because is it really us
To be afraid?

Lucy Townley (11)
St John The Baptist School, Kingfield

One Second, That's All

I'm drowning in this sea
You've infected my brain
One little thing
Makes me go insane
I'm serious.

I look back and realise, is it really that bad?
Will it affect me tomorrow?
Well,
It's my life, not yours
My profile.

Every minute, someone's life is taken away
Snatched
Broken
And I'm complaining
One little tear
Boy, I'm lucky to be here
Thump, thump, thump!
Silence
Life is too short
Appreciate it.

One second of your day you can smile
Make someone's week
That's only one second of your life
Five words, that's all

Now look at the bigger picture
And your complaining.

Madelyn Jane Pattison (12)
St John The Baptist School, Kingfield

The Derby

When the crowd comes to the stadium
When they enter the scene of metal titanium
'Cause you know who's playing
There is no delaying.

When the players are waving
All the crowd are swaying
Of the bad fans there
The players should take care.

It is lit, the flair
There is excitement in the air
There is a bad foul
And the player screams, "Ow!"

So now we shouldn't fight like warriors
We strive to be glorious
The derby of Manchester
Manchester United and Manchester City
If no one wins, it's a pity.

We all know who's going to win
Manchester United
So Manchester City fans should just throw their scarves in the bin!

Tunbosun Yusuf (12)
St John The Baptist School, Kingfield

Try

What type of person are you?
What do you like to watch?
What do you like to do?
Whatever it is,
For whatever reason,
Whatever you hide,
Let people see your friendly side,
In any situation, do it,
With no regret,
It'll be nice as long as you admit,
I know it's hard,
I know it's tough,
If other people judge,
If you trip, it's okay,
You will find your path again,
Don't look back at your pain,
Follow your dream, follow your way,
So try,
Don't cry,
Because one day, you'll fly,
Higher than other people,
Nothing will fall apart,
She loves you with all her heart,
Because you're perfect, just the way you are.

Dafne Lalli (11)
St John The Baptist School, Kingfield

Tennis

I start this poem with a
Bit of my passion
Tennis is what I love
To me, it is the new fashion.

I love tennis, it is kind of my thing
Playing five times a week
It is my coil spring.

Tennis makes you healthy
It keeps you nice and fit
Especially when you have a long hit.

Back and forth, over the net
We take a battering
For game and set.

You hate us when
We go into the net
It's not our fault
When you lose the set.

You win the game
You win the set
With heavy top spin
Over the net.

If you ever end up at
West Byfleet Tennis Club

You will see me there
With a tennis ball tub.

Jacob Tierney (12)
St John The Baptist School, Kingfield

Beauty May Not Remain

Gracefully walking,
Humble but threatened,
Quickly striding away,
Blood may drip,
But yet no mercy,
As the gun is lifted up,
What was once joy is now sadness,
As all hope is destroyed.

Many more face the very pain,
Over and over again,
What was once happiness is now worry,
Fear and a heartbreaking time,
We may not care,
But when we see,
Their pale faces lying,
On the thick, green floor full of sadness,
We feel guilt.

Fewer and fewer remain,
What we thought would be magnificent,
Fades away as the stunning beauty,
Turns into blood dripping,
Faces being washed away,
After all this...
What did we gain?

Peter Vincent (11)
St John The Baptist School, Kingfield

My Love

When you're gone, it's like life has ended
And when you're back, it's like my wounds are mended
You are my absolute everything
And I need you more than anything.

You are the only one for me
I really need no one else, you see
Your beautiful face is the perfect shape
And you stay in my mind every day.

I will be there for you through thick and thin
And we are so alike, you are almost my twin
It's like our brains work the same way
And will be together until we are old and grey.

I am constantly thinking about you
And you stick in my head, like glue
When I saw your ocean-blue eye,
I knew our love would never die.

Amy Lobb (11)
St John The Baptist School, Kingfield

Pollution

This planet once green,
Now filled with grey steam,
The lovely trees with emerald-green leaves
Are slowly,
Slowly falling into a deep,
Dark,
Pit.

The future is as black as darkness,
No brightness when awake
And gloominess will swallow whole
This world
That we have destroyed,
We made this mess,
Only we
Are responsible for this disaster
And now we may pay,
By never seeing the light of day
Again.

The lovely beaches once all blue,
All the rubbish to the sea blew,
All the creatures of the magic kingdom,
They are scared,
Lonely,

Lost.

All because of us.

Sofia Victoria Falcon Morin (12)
St John The Baptist School, Kingfield

Books... Books... Books...

Just sat down, exhausted, feeling like a crook,
Bad day at school or someone gave you a dirty look?
The best, most wonderful medicine for that is a book.

Thick books, thin books, books with fairies,
Books with Captain Hook,
Funny books, textbooks and just about any, I say,
Any book can brighten your day.

Opening the first page and launch,
Catapulted into a vivid world of treachery,
A newspaper report on the crime of the century,
A diary from the war, a devastating memory.

Finishing my book
And up I rise again,
Now feeling like a captain,
No longer like a crook,
And all I needed
Was a book.

Isla Kelly (11)
St John The Baptist School, Kingfield

My Cat

So lithe, so nimble, so graceful are you
Somehow, you're off the radar - like a spy
So unexpected, no one ever knew
You could be so sneaky, so smart, so sly.

You shine so bright, no, better yet, you glow
Like the moon and stars of a cloudless night
Mysteriously, your beauty does show
Those eyes - they almost create their own light.

Yet, it's common for you to disappear
One second you're here, the next you are not
Always missing when someone wants you near
Is this all a part of your secret plot?

Keep in mind you are a cat, my shrewd friend
I will remind you 'til the very end.

Pearl Alighieri (11)
St John The Baptist School, Kingfield

School

School, school is really cool
Except those bully fools,
The teachers that make you laugh,
The teachers that make you mad.

I like English because of the poetry,
Especially those that are limericks and stories,
PE is really physical
And computer coding is quite magical.

History is just the future and the past,
Geography is about the world around us,
Science is about the human body and chemicals,
Plus how you form twins to be identical.

Maths is really boring
Because of the topics we're learning,
I like art because I am never late,
Also, the colours I make with paint.

Godwin Saiju Dominic (11)
St John The Baptist School, Kingfield

My Family In Australia

I have lots of family in Australia
My nan who is caring
And doesn't like swearing
My pa who is funny
And loves to eat honey
My brother who's a tease
And I love to please
My cousins who are sneaky
And very, very cheeky
My uncle who is cool
Never, ever cruel
My auntie who's sweet
And always gives us treats
We all go down to the sapphire sea
To play when we are free
When we are on the coast
We all like having roasts
When the sun is scorching
We all go bodyboarding
And at night
We are all snuggle tight
Waiting for the day
So we can go and play.

Ella Martin (11)
St John The Baptist School, Kingfield

Nature

Sometimes I go,
To places I only know,
Forests of green
And a clear blue stream.

Slowly, I glide,
Pushing off of the side,
Through the vast, cold water,
Next to Mother Nature's daughter.

All the colours around
Makes the area very vibrant,
Leaving the landscape with a sound
Of pure and perfect silence.

A voice cries,
"It's coming!"
Creating a domino effect
Of disorder, disturbance and distress.

Swirling and whirling,
As lustrous as sterling,
Throwing all life in the air,
But as they say, let nature take its course.

Alyshea Lee (12)
St John The Baptist School, Kingfield

Why Cheat?

People dive
To get the chance
For that glory goal
But why?

It's clearly cheating
When the ref
Doesn't see
That's not fair
So why?

Is this cheating
Or is it just tactics?
Fail the pass
Still
Why?

This will start a fight
Of course, it will
So just play football
Without this silly nonsense
Then there'll be no 'why'.

All it will do is show you're a cheat
Even if you score
'Cause you'll set a reputation for your team
Not a good one, so...
Why?

Lola Leeming (12)
St John The Baptist School, Kingfield

The Soldiers Of Bullying

He is the jester at lunch,
With knives and stones thrown at his chest,
She is their gossip behind the hand.

They are the shared smirks,
As they dodge the bullets of words.

The hall is a torture chamber,
The playground is the battlefield,
The classroom is a death camp.

They are wounded soldiers,
Coming home from devastation,
But the comments still swirl
Around their head like a million
Cries.

Don't forget the soldiers of bullying
As they trek alone through the war
Because they cannot stand alone.

Orla Cook (11)
St John The Baptist School, Kingfield

Serve

Wearing their honourable badge
And their much cared for boots
They are the army
And they serve us.

As they crouch in a bush
Or load up their gun, they know
They serve our country.

As they jump from a plane
Or pack their bags, they know
Any day could be their last.

As they put themselves in danger's hands
Loyal like a dog they know, they do it for us
Not for themselves.

Parading, shooting, driving, diving, helping, sniping
Leading, policing, aiding, hiding, camping, thinking
...Serving...

Joseph Duggan (12)
St John The Baptist School, Kingfield

The Eon Typewriter

It clicks and it clammers,
Its old, rusty hammers,
As it inks the page for most of its days.
The keys are pressed
As it moves its best.
As the carriage moves along
Like a raging steam train of creativity
At the best of its ability
Inking similies, metaphors, adjectives
Verbs and punctuation
In perfect organisation.
Using the wide range of words
In a process of elimination
The noise of miniature metal workers
With not one
A shirker
As it lies on its favourite oak desk
Waiting to write its next burlesque.

Ben Turner (11)
St John The Baptist School, Kingfield

A Guinea Pig Life

I run around my cage all day
My cuteness takes their breath away
My owners feed me a lot of food
And when it's all gone, we're in a great mood
Me and my buddy, we always like to play
Bashing, bumping and biting, but in a friendly way.

In the morning, having hardly slept at all,
I wake up my owners with a deafening call
Which is an ear-piercing squeak, which you might think is quiet
However, you are mistaken, but why don't you try it?
Test it out, you will not regret
They really are the most incredible pet.

Jessica Bull (12)
St John The Baptist School, Kingfield

The Race

Bang!
The race is on
Shoving, nudging, pushing our way to the front
The sharp, cold air prickles my skin.

Thud!
My heart pounding
Breathing, panting, the tiredness slows my legs down
My bright orange T-shirt drips with sweat.

Cheer!
The crowd roaring
Clapping, cheering, will we win? Legs push harder
My focused mind stares at the finish.

Whoosh!
Poetry in motion
We passed another and another on the final straight
I smile in agony and delight.

William FitzGibbon (11)
St John The Baptist School, Kingfield

Friendship

Friends will stay with you forever
You won't always see them but you know they're there
You can count on them whenever
And one day, they'll show you that they really care.

They will comfort you when you're upset
They will make you laugh and smile
When you're down, they will make you forget
Your troubles that were worthwhile.

They will have your back in tough times
They will defend you at all costs
This is what a dream friend would be
This is what a true friend means to me.

Ruby Synan (12)
St John The Baptist School, Kingfield

Homeless People

Hollywood Walk of Fame
They may not have a family name
Always trying to aim
Higher
Trying to find a buyer
Just to get through life
They may have a knife
But they may not have a wife
It may be hard
When there are loads of blowhards
But just try to get out of the situation
There may be an occasion
When it is cold
You, you have just got to be bold
Get off the streets
Find something to eat
And don't end up on the Hollywood Walk of Fame,
Ever, ever
Again.

Poppy Tilbury (12)
St John The Baptist School, Kingfield

Imagination

You could be a dinosaur dancing with some toads,
You could be a wizard trying to tame a ferocious dragon,
You could be a tower watching nature grow,
You could even be Indiana Jones discovering the green of
the wild.

Oh, the imagination of a child,
Watch it grow, watch it learn, watch it play,
How we laughed and laughed,
The memories we made.

But alas, imagination will soon fade,
The beauty of the child's mind
Will die out,
For imagination will eventually corrode...

James Harte (12)
St John The Baptist School, Kingfield

Arctic Jungle

The snow splinters down, falling down onto a blanket of snow
They stare into the midnight sky at the roadside houses, coughing and snarling like a wolf howling in the night sky
Skies shuffle, mouths cough and ice hangs from the tips of the skies
The cars snarl and dustbins shiver in the night sky
The houses stand proudly like a statue
Streetlights bare in their white blanket
The lake is like a soft blanket when you skate
The bells ting in a rhythmic beat
The lights glisten in the night sky.

Sam Leahy (12)
St John The Baptist School, Kingfield

Memories

His eyes were like the ocean
They were full of life,
The memories playing together
In the wildlife,
We would never strife.

I miss being in your arms,
We would laugh and play in farms,
He was extraordinary,
His soft voice,
Kind-hearted, yet downhearted.

Days go by,
My tears dry,
When I feel blue,
The air of melancholy surrounds me,
I think of you,
Our hopes and dreams,
I wish you were here,
I miss you, Grandpa.

Stephanie Jardim (11)
St John The Baptist School, Kingfield

Lucy, Queen Of Cats

Your jet-black fur coat
Your razor-sharp, knife-like claws
Your golden, emerald eyes.

You're here by my side
When it's grey outside
I love you to bits
As I give you treats.

Oh, beautiful feline
Who tears down my washing line
You decimate my sofa chair
And rip my teddy bear.

Your satisfying purr
As I stroke your soft fur
And as you give me a nose kiss
You gently carry me along in a moment of bliss.

Ethan Cinnirella (11)
St John The Baptist School, Kingfield

Goal

The whistle goes,
As the pitch glows,
Under the glare of the bright lights.

The fans cheer,
As the goal draws near,
The striker taking the ball in his stride.

The defenders lunge,
Watching the striker plunge,
They're giving a penalty!

The ball is on the spot,
As the player makes a plot,
Where will he shoot?

The player shoots
And the crowd hoots,
The goalie makes himself big.

Goal!

Isaac Whiddett (11)
St John The Baptist School, Kingfield

Driving

From the screeching of the tyres,
To the enquiries of the drivers,
To the tracks over the mires,
I love the chance to drive.

Whether karts outside,
Or the simulators to drive,
It's the most fun thing to do.

I wish I could do it all Monday,
Maybe until Sunday,
Forever would be great too.

I wish for days without any rain,
To race around the track,
To beat my best time and leave,
My old best time to die.

Harry Wales (12)
St John The Baptist School, Kingfield

Football

The pitch looks like a battlefield ready for war,
Eleven against eleven are ready to score,
The whistle blows, the intensity rises,
The first crunching tackle energises,
The free kick drifts into the box,
Our lightning fast striker onto it like a fox,
The ball strikes the back of the net, the team in elation,
Let's get back to the halfway line in anticipation,
The game is over, we win 2-0,
The supporters say it was like watching Brazil.

Mason Richard Reeves (11)
St John The Baptist School, Kingfield

Is There Any Hope?

Emotionless,
The red balloon drifts away,
Saying it's last goodbyes,
Leaving my heart in despair,
I gave it my trust,
But now it has left me in its must.
The only colour in my life is gone!
Only dullness,
No happiness,
I had my hopes,
Now I will have to learn to cope.
Is there any hope left?
But now when I think,
I realise there is more
Than only this light
Right in front of me.

Jessica Hillier (12)
St John The Baptist School, Kingfield

Music

Music is part of every life
It's a material that's very essential
It was there all the time
It was always existential.

It's always good for my ears
I don't mind if it's good or bad
Because I know it will never disappear
And it will always cheer me up.

Music could be anywhere
Underwater or in the air
Music is not a feeling or an object
It's every single one of them.

Bartek Julian Radecki (12)
St John The Baptist School, Kingfield

War

War is a terrible thing
People scared, nowhere to go
Their hearts are cold
We are left out in the cold.

Death, darkness
As far as I can see
Why here, why now, why this?
Stop this... please.

They are hungry, they are in a mess
They are in distress
It's long, you want it to stop
Run quick, go, go, go, the bomb is about to blow...

Markus Majewski (11)
St John The Baptist School, Kingfield

Friendship

Friendship is endless, tremendous
Friends guide you in the darkness
Accept you for what you are.

They make you stronger
They give you hope!

Pick you up when you fall down
They're there for you no matter what
True friends are proud of you, never let you down.

With true friends by your side
No one can bring you down.

Angelica Caruso (11)
St John The Baptist School, Kingfield

Love Of Reading

She flies on the magic chair,
Then ends up in a crime scene,
Her love of reading never ends,
She loves to read all sorts.

It takes her places never been,
To characters that were never seen,
She meets the eighth king, Henry,
The kings and queens of the past
And when the stories come to an end,
She's really, really sad.

Milana Oziunaite (11)
St John The Baptist School, Kingfield

Beloved

She loved him,
He loved her,
When strong,
When weak,
When bad,
When good,
In downpour,
In snow and sun,
They loved him,
Away,
Away,
On the ferry,
He was gone,
From her,
She loved her horse,
Her horse loved her.

Evie Neary (12)
St John The Baptist School, Kingfield

Life Is Like Basketball

Life is like playing basketball
Dribble, run, walk, jump and shoot
Play without a ball and a goal
And the game will be pointless
So keep an eye on the ball and focus on the goal
Dribble, sweat, give energy and effort
And play with enthusiasm and pride.

Ryan Whelan (12)
St John The Baptist School, Kingfield

Racism

People walking around,
Different cultures,
Different languages,
Judging others on the way they look or speak,
Not on their real personality.

Giving people labels, black or white,
That's not right,
We are all equal.

Eliana Alongi (12)
St John The Baptist School, Kingfield

Our True Selves

We are all the same
Don't let us always take the blame
Why judge us on our sexuality, nationality or our rationality?
Just focus on our personality
Whether we're funny or nice
Whether we're kind or polite.

Keith Hilary Buscaglia (12)
St John The Baptist School, Kingfield

My Annoying Brother!

My annoying brother,
Different from others,
Never, ever leaving his bedroom,
Unless he needs his food,
He is always moaning at me
And he absolutely loves his PS4,
But I still love him.

Francesca Olivia Shaw (11)
St John The Baptist School, Kingfield

Winter

A haiku poem

A blanket of snow
Covering the bare, grey trees
Spreading chills on Earth.

Molly Walsh (11)

St John The Baptist School, Kingfield

Palindrome Mindset

Escape is a mistake
So don't tell yourself
You're upset and can cause change
Subtle droplets hopeful and inert
We're the riverbanks and bed
You're not the elected pilot, and even if
The first cold
Could spark a match or catch
Snow on the sharp side
Rain can't wash away the mud, the blood
So don't think that
If you're the first to fall, they'll follow.

Single shoe fibres can't escape what steps, but
You cling to our branches as
Leaves, purposeful until jettisoned and spent
It's impossible to wait until the master
Leads you to disaster
Reading down to ignore the advice.

Edward Coutts (14)
The Judd School, Tonbridge

261

Dying Of Dementia

He is lying on a hospital bed
Dying, dying of dementia
He can't remember me or my family
Dying, dying of dementia
He can't swallow now his insides are hollow
Dying, dying of dementia.

He is gasping for breath and here comes death
Dying, dying of dementia
Now his eyes close and now he holds a rose
Dying, dying of dementia.

There is an aura of grief as people lay down their memorial
wreath
Dying, dying of dementia
Although physical memories go wrong, the love will stay
strong
Loving, loving, united because of dementia.

Daniel Rowe (13)
The Judd School, Tonbridge

The Unwilling Worker

They had lasted as long as the last lot
He tried to forget their screams, but he could not
Their faces followed him everywhere he went
Despite his best efforts, he could never repent.

He was simply following an instruction
He took the job without a thought about the destruction
Of family, friends and human lives
Or the shrieking creation of agonising cries.

He could never leave his deathly post
He could only dream about the shimmering coast
Because that was where he wanted to be
Escaped, peaceful and blissfully free.

Seb Graham (14)
The Judd School, Tonbridge

Anti-Semitism

I am here to tell you about
A form of racism
The problem that is
Anti-Semitism.

Many people deny they were
Victims of fascism
Many decades ago, still
Anti-Semitism.

But it exists this very day
That same baleful schism
Between some and them
Anti-Semitism.

If we fight for what is right, then
I have optimism
That soon there won't be
Anti-Semitism.

We must strive to befriend those who
Follow Judaism
We must have peace, stop
Anti-Semitism.

Peter Blunt
The Judd School, Tonbridge

YoungWriters®
Est. 1991

YOUNG WRITERS INFORMATION

We hope you have enjoyed reading this book – and that you will continue to in the coming years.

If you're a young writer who enjoys reading and creative writing, or the parent of an enthusiastic poet or story writer, do visit our website **www.youngwriters.co.uk**. Here you will find free competitions, workshops and games, as well as recommended reads, a poetry glossary and our blog. There's lots to keep budding writers motivated to write!

If you would like to order further copies of this book, or any of our other titles, then please give us a call or visit **www.youngwriters.co.uk**.

Young Writers
Remus House
Coltsfoot Drive
Peterborough
PE2 9BF
(01733) 890066
info@youngwriters.co.uk

Join in the conversation!
Tips, news, giveaways and much more!

f YoungWritersUK   **y** @YoungWritersCW